STUDIES IN BRITISH GOVERNMENT

STUDIES IN
BRITISH GOVERNMENT

BY

N. H. BRASHER, M.A.

LONDON
MACMILLAN & CO LTD
NEW YORK · ST MARTIN'S PRESS
1965

MACMILLAN AND COMPANY LIMITED
St Martin's Street London WC 2
also Bombay Calcutta Madras Melbourne

THE MACMILLAN COMPANY OF CANADA LIMITED
70 Bond Street Toronto 2

ST MARTIN'S PRESS INC
175 Fifth Avenue New York 10010 NY

PRINTED IN GREAT BRITAIN

Preface

IN subject matter this book ranges over several issues of current constitutional interest. It follows broadly the syllabuses set by examining boards for pupils studying government. The growing emphasis on general studies for both the Arts and Science student should lead to a closer study of the workings of government by the non-specialist also, and it is hoped that the book may be of value for this purpose. Whatever else students may become they will certainly be citizens, and knowledge of the present-day institutions of government is still not a universal characteristic in schools.

The emphasis in the book, however, is on ideas, changing habits of government, and possible reforms, rather than on the provision of a mass of factual information. It is intended to be an accompaniment, or sequel, to the textbooks, a bridge between them and the study of specialist books. Much of it is directed towards the stimulation of discussion which forms such a large part of advanced work in particular. An outline and theme are given at the beginning of each chapter so that its pattern may be quickly grasped. Many of the issues discussed are controversial. While it would have been possible to prepare a cautious and uncommitted assessment of present-day tendencies in government, I felt that this would blunt the critical approach which the book is designed to foster. I have thought it best to put forward my own views positively, not only in the expectation, but even a little in the hope, that the views of readers may frequently differ sharply from my own. I hope, too, that the ideas put forward will rouse sufficient thought to lead students to make constructive use of the specialist books in order to support or reconsider their own views. If this happens a worthwhile purpose will have been achieved. To help this process I have added a book-list with comments. My own debt to many of the authors mentioned there will be very plain.

A short book of this kind, dealing with a variety of important topics, will inevitably have many omissions. There are also several issues, potentially rich in controversy, to which it has only been possible to make fleeting reference, though this may sometimes be

a sufficient starting point for argument. Most of the book was
written during 1962 and subsequent events are only briefly mentioned. What has concerned me chiefly, however, is less the pursuit
of topicality for its own sake than the examination of recent trends
in government which seem to be of permanent importance. In this
respect the book may also be of interest to the general reader.
Readers will discover a strong emphasis, for instance, on the growth
of central direction by modern governments. The fact that this is a
familiar theme makes it no less important. The formal barriers to
the authority of the Government in Britain are negligible; it is all
the more important, therefore, where public opinion is the only
ultimate restraint on Government action, to know which of the
traditional rights are expendable, and which are not. Making the
distinction is difficult, especially in the changing conditions and
emergencies of modern times, but there can be few matters of
greater importance. It would be one of the sadder ironies of our
history if the freedoms which have been so vigorously won and
defended should wither away through cynicism and ignorance of
their worth. Fortunately Britain has nothing worse to fear at the
moment than the benevolent despotism of the Cabinet or the involuntary dictatorship imposed largely by the pressure of outside
events. Yet it would be as well to remember that this is not the full
extent of the risk to be faced in a country whose traditional flexibility of constitutional habits is not an unmitigated advantage,
especially when there are pressures on the central Government to
tighten its control. Considerable attention has been given in the
book, therefore, to matters which are symptomatic of the more
authoritarian approach of modern governments.

Those who are familiar with the workings of government will
not, however, expect a consistent pattern to emerge. In the early
chapters, in particular, there are frequent references to the greater
centralisation of modern times. Yet in the chapter on local government it is apparent that, except in the unlikely event of the Government having intentions of the most Machiavellian subtlety, local
authorities have been given, or will be given, greater freedom than
they had before. Beyond this, the movement towards self-government of the new Commonwealth countries could, in a different
way, be regarded as an outstanding example of decentralisation. It
has not proved to be possible, therefore, to find a single theme
which can be said to characterise all aspects of the work of a modern

British Government. In a country where government is based largely on empirical methods the absence of a consistent approach is the less surprising.

Adequate acknowledgment to those who have helped in different ways in the preparation of this book would be impossible. I must, however, give particular thanks to Dr. D. G. Southgate, lecturer in Modern History at the University of St. Andrews, and to Mr. P. D. Whitting, G.M., B.A., who, until his retirement, was senior history master at St. Paul's School. Their judicious blending of encouragement and criticism has been of the greatest assistance to me. Imperfections which remain are my own, but I am well aware how many more there would have been without the help of these two advisers. I have also received very generous information from the Electoral Reform Society and from the research department of the Labour Party, although, as it happens, on the specific issues concerned I differed from their views. Mr. Malcolm Shaw, the Director of Studies and Information of the Hansard Society for Parliamentary Government, the staffs of Her Majesty's Stationery Office, and of the Orpington and Bromley Libraries have been most helpful in the verification of references. My publishers have been admirably patient; so, too, have been my wife and family who have contrived to give me the peace without which the book could not have been written at all.

N. H. B.

Contents

I

The Monarchy

Decline of monarchies. The flexibility of the British monarchy illustrated from its historical development. Its powers and limitations, with examples from nineteenth- and twentieth-century history. The monarchy does not need to be justified simply by its practical political duties. Value of the monarch's social duties. Relationship to the Commonwealth countries.

THEME: The powers of the British monarch are neither dangerous nor superfluous.

In a world where social upheavals have become commonplace the power of the British monarchy to survive makes it of special interest. Its existence, rooted deeply in the past, is based on the concept of a definite hierarchy in society of which it is the apex. It might seem, therefore, to represent a view of society which is anathema to the social reformer. Criticism of it is to be expected and involves no novelty in itself, for the institution of monarchy has been subjected to the most violent attacks for over three hundred years. The events of the seventeenth century culminating in the Bill of Rights of 1689 marked the fiercest phase of the conflict, but ripples of the controversy continued to be felt until the end of the nineteenth century. By the beginning of the twentieth century, however, the Crown had tacitly accepted the position that for almost all practical purposes personal intervention by the monarch in politics was undesirable. This largely removed the long-standing grievance against despotic or arbitrary actions by the monarch, but has led to criticisms of a different kind, that, as the political powers of the monarch have dwindled away almost to vanishing point, the retention of a non-functional institution is merely a social pretence out of keeping with the modern world, like medieval battlements on a New York skyscraper.

This criticism that the monarchy has become redundant in

modern times attracts a certain measure of support. It is true that it is no longer possible to defend the institution of monarchy with the mystical arguments used in the time of James I, when the theory of the Divine Right of Kings to govern made criticism on a par with impiety. That theory was violently discredited when, on January 30th, 1649, in Whitehall, the head of Charles I was displayed to the crowd attending the execution. A more significant stage still was reached on January 21st, 1793, when the guillotine severed the neck of Louis XVI amid cries of 'Vive la nation!', for to the French Revolutionary leaders the movement against the monarchy had become an idealistic campaign. The Parliamentarians in England were waging a struggle against a monarch: the early French Revolutionaries wanted to wage an international struggle against monarchy, and their influence was correspondingly greater. The precedent, once set, was swiftly imitated. Monarchs were no longer sacrosanct, and revolution continued to find new victims. In France, revolutions in 1830 and 1848 disposed first of Charles X, then of Louis Philippe. In 1848 there was a brief experience of Republican government before the monarchical principle was revived under Napoleon III, but in 1870, following the Prussian defeat of France at the battle of Sedan, the monarchy was finally discredited and Republican government has been adopted ever since. Spain, having witnessed the deposition of Queen Isabella in 1868, reverted to a monarchy only to dispense with it in 1931 when King Alfonso XIII was deposed. In July, 1918, the Tsar of Russia, who had governed with the kind of despotism reminiscent of the Bourbons before 1789, was murdered at Ekaterinburg in central Russia, as a result of the 1917 Russian Revolution. A few months later his recent enemy the Kaiser was in exile in Holland, with theatrical demands being made by some of his opponents that he should be hanged. Along with the Kaiser there had disappeared the Austrian Emperor and the whole penumbra of minor German Kings. In modern Italy the monarchy after years of humiliating subordination in the Fascist state was replaced by a republic in 1946. Altogether the Royal casualty list makes impressive reading. Apart from Britain no major European power has retained a monarchical system, and though some of the smaller powers have done so, the hostility of many nations to such a system is only too clear.

Critics who point out, therefore, that Britain, in retaining a monarchy, lags behind many of its Continental contemporaries in constitutional development, have substantial evidence at their disposal. The argument based on comparison with Continental practice deserves consideration, for imitation is an accepted feature in constitutional practice, and the constitutional habits of our neighbours are not necessarily bad ones because we failed to invent them ourselves. There are, however, other factors to consider. Historically, the British monarchy, at least since the Civil War, can be compared with advantage with the European monarchies. It has greater continuity than imperialism or monarchy in France or Germany; it is stronger than the Italian monarchy of Mussolini's time; it rules over a more united country than Imperial Austria, or Spain in the inter-war years; it is free of the vices of absolutism of Tsarist Russia. All these kingships contained the seeds of their own destruction. If the British monarchy revealed failings similar to those which led to the abolition of these monarchies in Europe then the argument by comparison would be more powerful. As it is, this has not been suggested, and to propose to abolish the monarchy simply because many of our neighbours have done so would be patently absurd.

The essential advantage which the British monarchy possesses over these Continental monarchies lies in its flexibility. Opposition to the principle of monarchy, or to particular aspects of its working, has led in the past to revolution, and to reduction of the monarch's powers. Yet the monarchy, apart from the brief interlude of 1649–60, has survived. Its authority no longer rests on Divine Right. It has become a constitutional monarchy dependent on Parliament for its powers, and even for its existence. There is now little danger of any abuse of power by the monarch. To understand why this is so it is necessary to trace the changing relationship between Parliament and the monarchy from the late seventeenth century onwards. In doing so, two facts of equal importance will emerge. One is the obvious point that Parliament has increasingly been able to establish its supremacy over the Crown; the second, complementary to this but less obvious, is that only a monarchy of a most flexible nature could have adapted itself to these changes. Moreover, this flexibility is not only significant in understanding the historical development of the monarchy; it could clearly have some bearing on its future development too. It is worth noting also that the changed relationship between Parliament and the monarchy has been brought about without a recurrence of the violence of the seventeenth century, yet also without such a complete suppression of the rights of the monarchy as to make it a nullity.

The terms imposed by Parliament in the Bill of Rights, following the abdication of James II, hedged the monarchy with restrictions which William III was bound to accept if he wished to establish his personal right to be a co-monarch with the lawful successor, his wife Mary, and to ensure Parliamentary support for his war with Louis XIV. These restrictions were based on the experiences of the century. They mark a vital change in that they assure the constitutional supremacy of Parliament in some spheres of government. Parliamentary sanction was required for the collection of taxes. The monarch was not to be a Roman Catholic, nor could he marry a Roman Catholic. The power which James II had exercised in favour of the Catholics to exempt them from the normal working of the laws, such as the Test Act of 1673, which had required acceptance of the fundamental doctrines of the Church of England by judges, mayors, and officers, was removed. Furthermore, the King was not to have a standing army in peace-time, a restriction imposed no doubt because of the Parliamentarians' recent memory of James II's menacing Irish levies stationed at Hounslow within comfortable distance of London. Parliamentary control of the army was shortly reinforced by the Mutiny Acts of 1689 and 1717 providing for the discipline of the army. The clauses of these Acts, particularly when coupled with Parliamentary control of the pay of men through the Army Estimates, made it impossible for the armed forces to continue in being without Parliamentary sanction. The Bill of Rights also secured freedom of speech and of debates on proceedings in Parliament. Again, recent events, such as the disagreements with Charles II and James II, played their part in the insertion of this clause. These restrictions, therefore, were devised as solutions to immediate problems, but they have remained as permanent features of the constitution. By means of these restrictions Parliament had already by 1689 partly removed the possibility of royal supremacy in the constitution. There were frequent references in the Bill of Rights to the fact that its provisions could not be altered 'save by Act of Parliament'. In 1701 a further decisive stage was reached when the Act of Settlement made it clear that as well as primogeniture (the right of the first-born to succeed) Parliamentary approval was also necessary to ensure legal succession to the throne. This had already been evident in practice in 1660 at the restoration of Charles II, and in 1688 with the choice of William and Mary as co-monarchs. Now, in making arrangements for the succession after the death of William, Parliament was giving statutory form to the principle that the royal title rests on Parliamentary approval, a background factor which was clearly of importance in recent times when Edward VIII decided to abdicate in 1936. The Act of Settlement also made it impossible for the King to remove judges from office. They held office 'quamdiu se bene gesserint', that is, so long as they fulfilled their functions with probity, and they could only be removed by a joint petition from the two Houses of Parliament.

The constitutional importance of these changes of the 1689–1701 period lies in the fact that the long-voiced claims of Parliament to play a continuous role in the process of government were now given a much more effective basis. This, in itself, was at least a potential limitation of royal influence, and as time went on it proved to be much more. Historians are rightly cautious about ascribing undue importance to single dates in history, but there are reasonable grounds for regarding 1689 as an exception. The Revolutionary Settlement clearly opened the way for the development of many of the features of the Parliamentary system which we now take for granted. Once regularity of meeting was assured then, very slowly, the need for party support, for a good working relationship between ministers and Parliament, and for collective responsibility for Ministerial actions was made clearer by sheer pressure of circumstances rather than by preconceived constitutional theories. The effect, in practice, of these changes was to reduce still further the extent of royal influence. They are, it may be noticed, concerned with matters of conventional usage rather than statutory limitations on the powers of the monarch, yet it could be held that it was the statutes of 1689 which gave the strongest impetus to the development of the modern constitutional relationship between Parliament and the monarchy. That the devisers of the Settlement themselves would have been astonished by its later consequences is one of the commonplaces of history.

Attention has been drawn to the slowness of constitutional change in Britain since 1689. This in itself has been an asset to the monarchy, since the strain on its adaptability has been less intense than in some of its Continental counterparts, for instance the French monarchy of the eighteenth century. Royal influence remained strong long after 1689, nor was this generally regarded as undesirable, still less unconstitutional. William III, in spite of the statutory limitations on his power, was still the active commander of the nation's forces in the field. He could still wage an unpopular war. He could still preside at meetings of ministers, and these indications of continuing royal power remained in force for many years to come. George II led British and Hanoverian troops into action at Dettingen in 1743. His zealous interest in Hanover led him at times to take a direct part in foreign policy, particularly during the war of the Austrian Succession. At home Carteret's dependence on royal support between 1742 and 1744, and George's exclusion of Pitt from the 1744 ministry on personal grounds, provide well-known instances of the extent of royal power at the time. Nor were these actions in the least unusual. George III's strongly formed views on measures and men are well known. His determination to subdue the American colonists, his decisive part in securing the defeat of the Fox-North coalition in 1783, and his action in choosing the Younger Pitt as chief minister, though the latter could not for a time command a majority in the House of Commons, are outstanding examples of the crucial importance still of the Crown influence. Patronage played a part in bolstering up the strength of the Crown, but this would not have been sufficient had there not been also a strong feeling among the many independently minded M.P.s that Crown activity, so long as it did not infringe the limits imposed by the Revolution Settlement, was entirely legitimate.[1]

Yet, alongside this view, based on well-established traditions, a newer one was growing up of greater significance for the future. This was the slow emergence of the idea of government by a Cabinet with some sense of collective responsibility. To be completely effective it needed the backing of the fully organised party support which is clearly lacking in the eighteenth century in spite of the efforts of the Treasury managers, the great landowners, and the extensive use of jobbery. In fact the most effective support, that given to the Younger Pitt, sprang not from self-interest nor from party policies, an anachronism anyway in the eighteenth century, but from admiration of his personal qualities. Whatever

[1] For a defence of George's actions see J. Steven Watson, *The Reign of George III., 1760–1815* (Oxford—Clarendon Press, 1960).

the basis of collective responsibility, however, as soon as there is evidence of its existence, no matter how tenuous, at that point it can be said that the exercise of royal power in the manner which had been customary up to the end of the eighteenth century is under immediate threat. Students of constitutional history will know better than to expect any change to be rapid, simple, or, in detail, continuous. George III was able to bring about the resignation of Pitt in 1801, for instance, over the question of Catholic Emancipation, and colleagues of Pitt continued to serve in the succeeding Addington ministry. There are later instances, too, of this negative control by the Crown on particular issues which roused strong feeling, such as George III's dispute with his ministers over Catholic Emancipation in 1807, and the dissolution of the Melbourne ministry in 1834, stemming partly from the personal antipathy of William IV for Lord John Russell, whom Lord Melbourne wished to make Leader of the House. Yet there is abundant evidence to show that as Cabinet Government gathered strength and Crown patronage declined, so the positive direction of policy passed almost entirely from the hands of the Crown. It is this long process which constitutes the Glorious Revolution rather than the so-called Glorious Revolution itself.

The change in atmosphere becomes clearly discernible in the reign of Queen Victoria. Much is made at times of the forcible views expressed by the Queen on matters of personality and policy. Her horror of radicals, her dislike for Gladstone and her attempts to oust him from party leadership, her antipathy to the Russians at the time of their war against Turkey; these and many other of her political foibles are well known. Nor was her influence by any means confined to the expression of opinion. As late as 1892, for instance, she was able on personal grounds to refuse to accept Sir Charles Dilke and Mr. Labouchere for any office, an action recalling the constitutional habits of the eighteenth century. On policy decisions too, she did not hesitate to state her opinions strongly, but it is open to argument that she was more active than influential especially after 1868. Joseph Chamberlain, for instance, whose radical views were as unpopular with the Queen as those of Fox had been with George III, was able to develop his distinguished career unmoved by royal displeasure. Gladstone, in the face of strong royal hostility, was able to be Prime Minister for a total period of over thirteen years, and to carry through policies which were anathema to the imperialist Queen. But it would be unjust to represent the Queen merely as a reactionary fractiously struggling against the accumulating pressure of constitutional custom. It is characteristic of the self-denying principle we have grown to expect from modern British monarchy that the reduction in royal influence after 1837 was caused not merely by the pressure of external events but also by voluntary withdrawal. N. Gash in *Politics in the Age of Peel* has drawn attention to the crucial importance of the Windsor by-election in 1845. Queen Victoria, supported and probably advised by Prince Albert, made it clear to Peel, then Prime Minister, that the practice by which the Crown had virtually secured the right of nomination to one of the Windsor seats would be discontinued. Writing after the interview to Sir William Fremantle, Peel said, 'The Queen does not wish to interfere in Elections and there is no separating in this matter the Court from the Sovereign.'[1] Admittedly the extension of the franchise and the growing strength of the collective-responsibility doctrine would in themselves have involved a considerable reduction in the opportunities for royal intervention in politics. Yet it was a good omen for the future sound relations between the monarchy and the government of the day that there had been this willingness on the part of the Crown to surrender some measure of its former influence. It is of incidental interest, perhaps, on this subject that while the opinionated views of Queen Victoria have been strongly assailed, by a curious reversal of attitude there have been occasional suggestions that it would be of value to the country if the monarch were less reticent in matters of opinion. It is arguable (though difficult to maintain) that, since the balance of the constitution has been upset in this century by the predominance of the Executive, there might be some advantage in the monarch advancing opinions which would gain in strength through her independence of party connection. These opinions would be the more valuable if they were based on the experience of a long reign.

It is evident that since 1689 the monarchy, through statute and custom, has been deprived of any effective means of exercising arbitrary power. Although this process owes more to usage than to law, it is usage based on strong sanctions. A monarch who challenged the authority of Parliament would find that the machinery of government would come to a standstill, that the Armed Forces

[1] N. Gash, *op. cit.*, p. 382 (Longmans, 1953).

could not continue in being, and that no revenue and no Civil List allowance would be forthcoming. In practice, long before any of these stages had been reached a recalcitrant monarch would have been removed and replaced by someone more amenable: this removal would be made the more certain by knowledge of the ultimate sanctions which Parliament has in reserve. Criticism of the present-day monarchy is based, therefore, less on the charge that it is dangerous than on the charge that it is useless. An examination of the functions of the Crown will show how much truth there is in this allegation.

It is true that the Queen, who is in name the Head of all the major functions of government, exercises for the most part purely nominal powers. Her connection with Parliament is primarily confined to the State Opening at the beginning of a session, and the granting of Royal Assent to Bills. No monarch since Queen Anne in 1708 has withheld this assent, and even then she was acting on the advice of her ministers. The danger of royal opposition is negligible. In addition, the extension of the franchise has removed the possibility for the Crown of intervening in Parliamentary affairs on behalf of the mass of the people against the class interests of representatives elected on a limited franchise, and often corruptly, for this was the state of affairs before the nineteenth-century Reform Bills. Now this reason, which might become merely a pretext, no longer applies. Furthermore, the long struggle for financial dominance between Crown and Parliament was decisively settled in favour of Parliament by the Bill of Rights in 1689. The grant of a Civil List has increased the Crown's dependence on Parliament. Direct participation in the affairs of Parliament of the kind practised regularly by George III, and occasionally by Queen Victoria, can be excluded. In this respect the monarch has become a spectator rather than a participant. She merely receives information about Parliamentary proceedings from the daily reports of the Vice-Chamberlain of the Household, and from the frequent visits by the Prime Minister.

Yet this passive role in Parliamentary affairs does not exhaust all the possibilities. The powers of the monarch in political affairs are severely circumscribed but they are not extinct. Bagehot's assessment of the nineteenth-century situation was that the monarch had three rights — 'the right to be consulted, the right to encourage, and the right to warn, and a King of great sense and sagacity would want no others'.[1] In fact, as has been seen, Queen Victoria was not content with this subordinate role. Vigorous partisanship of this kind no longer applies in the twentieth century; it would be neither necessary nor welcome so long as circumstances are normal; but everlasting normality is too much to expect in the fluid world of politics where personal strains and the speedy onset of crises in modern times may at any time present novel or peculiar constitutional difficulties.

Even in the twentieth century, when monarchs have willingly abandoned the political influence freely used by Queen Victoria, there have been occasions when royal initiative in politics has become desirable. One instance was the crisis of 1910 over the Parliament Bill. George V was confronted on this occasion with a situation where his prerogative powers needed to be used with the greatest care. He had to decide whether to promise the Liberal Government to create sufficient peers to ensure that the Parliament Bill would pass through the House of Lords against the opposition of the Conservative Lords. In addition, he had to decide on the propriety of a dissolution. There had already been one dissolution in 1910 to allow public opinion to be expressed on the deadlock between Lords and Commons over the 1909 Budget. These decisions were far from nominal, and the personal attitude of the King was a strong factor in the situation. In fact, King George V agreed both to dissolve Parliament and to create enough peers to ensure the passage of the bill if the Liberals won the election. Both decisions were wise, but the essential point is that in the intense pressures to which the monarch was subjected during this violent controversy other decisions were possible without infringing constitutional usage. The Leader of the Conservative Opposition, Mr. Balfour, had suggested, for instance, before King Edward VII's death, that the monarch should refuse to give a dissolution and should ask the Opposition to form a Government. In short, there was enough uncertainty in the situation to make the element of personal decision by the monarch a reality. George V's personal influence was again experienced in 1931. After consultation with the party leaders, made necessary by the financial crisis and the instability of the Labour Government, he was advised to propose the formation of a National Government with ministers drawn from the main parties and led by Ramsay MacDonald. This sug-

[1] *The English Constitution*, p. 111 (Fontana Library Edition, 1963).

gestion was accepted by the King, and MacDonald, though many of his Labour colleagues left him, accordingly formed a new coalition government. This is an important instance, since it illustrates one of the fundamental duties of the monarch, often overlooked, namely the vitally important function of ensuring continuity of government. With the Labour Government divided over the measures necessary to recover from the financial crisis, the first consideration of the monarch had to be the establishment of a more stable ministry. King George may not have initiated the idea of a coalition government but his decision to accept or reject the idea was clearly of some consequence. Lord Morrison in *Government and Parliament* is critical of the decision which was taken,[1] but he accepts the fact that there was no breach of constitutional propriety in the King's action. It is true that the decision was damaging to the Labour Party, which found itself seriously divided, but it was essential in the financial crisis of 1931 to secure a Government which could maintain majority support in the House of Commons, and a National Government was able to do this. The electorate's support for this view was amply demonstrated at the General Election held shortly afterwards. Although monarchs have given advice on political matters since then, the 1931 crisis was the last occasion on which the monarch has had a major role in the formation of a Government. The recurrence of a similar situation remains possible however.

The monarch's duty to ensure continuity of government and to choose a Prime Minister, as George V chose Ramsay MacDonald, is thus demonstrably of some significance still. A further reminder of its potential importance came in the appointment of Mr. Macmillan as Prime Minister in 1957. Sir Anthony Eden (now Lord Avon) had resigned owing to ill-health accentuated by the strain of the brief campaign against Egypt over the Suez Canal dispute. In normal circumstances the Conservative Party naturally takes pains to groom a successor to the Prime Minister, as Eden had been prepared, for instance, to take over from Sir Winston Churchill. Events had moved so swiftly, however, that there was a distinct element of doubt over the succession to the leadership. Mr. Macmillan and Mr. Butler were the two leading candidates. In a situation of this kind the monarch, with a reputation for impartiality, may well be ideally suited for choosing a Prime Minister.

[1] *Ibid.*, pp. 77–80.

Queen Elizabeth had then reigned for only five years. She was advised in her choice by Lord Salisbury, who then led the Conservatives in the House of Lords, by Sir Winston Churchill, and conjecturally by Lord Woolton, the Conservative Party ex-chairman; Cabinet opinion was also sounded. It might be expected that the advice of Sir Anthony Eden, as outgoing Prime Minister, would be an important factor in the choice of a successor, but this does not appear to have been so. Clearly, in an instance of this kind, the advice of senior statesmen will weigh heavily with a young monarch though, constitutionally, the decision remains her own. It does not follow, however, that the element of real personal decision by the monarch can be regarded as totally excluded for all time. An experienced monarch confronted by political deadlock could well provide a means of resolving it.[1]

The examples given show that there are still some situations demanding a degree of initiative and personal decision by the monarch in political matters. Nor do these examples by any means exhaust the possibilities of royal intervention. Sir Ivor Jennings points out in *The Queen's Government* that if a defeated Prime Minister refused to resign, in spite of a vote of no confidence, the Queen would resolve the deadlock by commissioning the Leader of the Opposition to form a new Government.[2] Acceptance of the conventions makes this situation unlikely, but it is desirable to have the constitutional mechanism available to deal with any emergency of this kind; this function the monarchy fulfils admirably. There is, furthermore, the special power vested in the monarch in relation to the dissolution of Parliament. Dissolution is normally ordered by the Sovereign on the advice of a Prime Minister, but it would be quite wrong to infer that the personal opinion of the monarch is never of any account in matters affecting the dissolution of Parliament. In his biography of George VI[3] Sir John Wheeler-Bennett has described very clearly the attitude of the King during the

[1] A deadlock of this kind could conceivably have developed in October, 1963, when there were several contenders for the succession to Mr. Macmillan as Prime Minister. If it had become clear that none of these contenders could form a Government, the Queen would have been entitled to ask Mr. Wilson, Leader of the Opposition, to do so. It would be rash to discount altogether the element of the monarch's personal opinion in such a situation.

[2] *Ibid.*, pp. 41–3.

[3] Sir John Wheeler-Bennett, *King George VI: his Life and Reign*, pp. 791–6.

1950–1 Labour administration when stability of government was severely hampered by the precarious majority held by the Labour Party. During this time the King's rights both to press for a dissolution, and, in certain circumstances, to refuse one were far from being merely academic matters. The King was about to undertake a tour to Australia and New Zealand, and was characteristically anxious as a conscientious monarch that a political crisis should not develop in his absence. This was a strong possibility, since the Labour majority was only six. It was of some relevance too that the King was aware of his own failing health and was anxious that his daughter should not be confronted with a political crisis immediately on her accession. King George VI, therefore, wrote to Mr. (now Lord) Attlee, sounding him on his intention to ask for a dissolution, and making it plain from the tone of the letter that there was urgent need to secure greater political stability than obtained at the time. Lord Attlee has since denied (in an article for the *Observer* of August 23rd, 1959) that he was pushed into asking for a dissolution by some pressure from the King. 'There is no substance in this, but the position of the King was one which I personally had to take into account.' In a situation of this kind royal advice is clearly not decisive. Lord Attlee speaking on B.B.C. television in February, 1963, stated that the strain on the health of Labour members helping to maintain the Government's slender majority was his predominant motive in seeking a dissolution. He was no doubt also influenced by the desire to secure the most politically opportune moment for the election. Yet if royal wishes were not decisive in 1951 neither were they negligible. Implicit in Lord Attlee's attitude is an acceptance of the fact that the monarch still retains a measure of responsibility for the maintenance of political stability. This is the fact which justifies King George's approach to Lord Attlee. It is also a reminder that the monarchy should not be regarded as if it were of no political consequence whatsoever.

Another aspect of the right of dissolution was also closely scrutinised in the 1950–1 period. This was the right of the monarch to refuse to grant a dissolution. The essence of the matter is contained in a letter written to *The Times* on May 2nd, 1950, by Sir Alan Lascelles, the Private Secretary to King George VI. This letter is quoted in the official biography of King George VI.[1] It states that no wise Sovereign would refuse to grant a dissolution

[1] Sir John Wheeler-Bennett, *op. cit.*, p. 775.

'unless he were satisfied that: (1) the existing Parliament was still vital, viable, and capable of doing its job; (2) a General Election would be detrimental to the national economy; (3) he could rely on finding another Prime Minister who could carry on his Government for a reasonable period with a working majority in the House of Commons'. Refusal by a monarch to grant a dissolution is clearly unlikely, more so in practice than the Lascelles letter suggests, but it is not impossible.[1] It is desirable for a monarch to seek advice on a matter of such importance, as King George VI did from Sir John Anderson in particular during the period described. Yet his own opinion may well be a factor in the final decision in the unusual, but not unique circumstances of the kind which prevailed in 1950-1. One further development which might have materialised, but which did not, is that the 1951 election might again have returned a Government without a working majority. King George VI and his advisers were ready for this eventuality, as is evident again in the official biography. The solution would have been a recommendation by the King for the formation of a National Government. The likely reactions of the leading politicians to this possibility had been assessed before the 1951 election took place, and had that election produced an indefinite result royal intervention with the object of securing a stable government by means of a coalition might well have taken place.

It is evident then that, constitutionally, the monarch is not merely a figure-head — the Crown is too closely concerned with the management of the steering-wheel for that comparison to be apt. Nevertheless, its powers of real decision would be reserved for quite exceptional situations, and there have been occasions in this century when royal wishes have been respectfully heard but ultimately overruled. As a legal concept the supreme authority in the country is the Crown-in-Parliament but, in general, it is the will of the elected Assembly which must prevail, and the pre-eminence of the Commons in practice has been accepted both by the monarch and the House of Lords in modern times. Queen Victoria's wish to avoid having Gladstone as Prime Minister was circumvented by the refusal of the other Liberals to accept the office. More recently it is clear from the private papers of King George VI, quoted in

---

[1] Cf. Lord Asquith's speech at the National Liberal Club, 1923 (Le May, *British Government 1914-53*, p. 155) for a justification of the monarch's right to refuse to accept a dissolution of Parliament.

his biography by Sir John Wheeler-Bennett, that the King had strong opinions over certain appointments. In 1940, King George made it very evident to Neville Chamberlain, at the period of his resignation, that he was strongly in favour of Lord Halifax succeeding as Prime Minister.[1] Chamberlain advised him that Churchill would be a better choice: this the King accepted, though with some reluctance. Again, although it has been asserted that royal influence was brought to bear over the appointment of Mr. Bevin rather than Sir Hugh Dalton to the post of Foreign Secretary in 1945,[2] this is denied by Lord Attlee who says in the *Observer* of August 23rd, 1959, that, although he naturally took into account the King's view which was very sound, 'it was not a decisive factor in my arrival at my decision.' Lord Morrison states in *Government and Parliament* that on two occasions he formed a different opinion from the King on the subject of reprieves for condemned persons.[3] In theory the grant of a reprieve is part of the Royal prerogative powers. In practice Lord Morrison, having listened respectfully to the King's views, decided that he could not agree, and it was Morrison's views which prevailed. The scope for royal initiative in policy is therefore narrowly circumscribed but not negligible. Furthermore, there is not the least risk of royal intervention, except on easily justifiable grounds, since the House of Commons by its control of finance, including the annual grants to the Royal Family from the Civil List, could easily bring government to a standstill in the highly improbable event of being confronted by dictatorial intervention by the monarch.

The remaining prerogative powers of the Crown have largely lost significance with the passage of time and the development of the doctrine of Ministerial Responsibility. The making of peace and war, the conduct of foreign affairs, the making of treaties, the appointment of judges, the granting of charters of incorporation, the award of the titles of honour, the headship of the Armed Forces, and the appointment of high officials, these are all prerogative powers which sprang from what used to be the direct personal authority of the monarch, but now these powers are delegated virtually in their entirety to the Ministers of the Crown. The monarch's prerogative power to create peers has had more recent significance. Until 1911 the Lords' power of absolute veto gave

---

[1] Sir John Wheeler-Bennett, *op. cit.*, pp. 443–4.   [2] *Ibid.*, p. 638.
[3] Lord Morrison, *Government and Parliament*, p. 81.

them, in a sense, constitutional supremacy. The monarch's power to create peers could therefore be of some political value, as it was in the 1910–11 disputes when King George V agreed to create sufficient peers to ensure the passage of the Parliament Act through the House of Lords. Once this Act was passed constitutional dominance passed to the Commons, and their position was further strengthened by the Parliament Act of 1949 reducing the Lords' power of veto to one year. Thus the necessity for royal intervention as it occurred in 1911 has largely passed away, and this aspect of the prerogative has also virtually lost any element of political significance.

If the justification of the monarchy rested merely on the occasional exercise of the prerogative powers it would still be an adequate defence of the institution. Political and constitutional crises do arise, as the earlier examples quoted show, and a monarch is better fitted to deal with them than a President, whose actions would inevitably be more vulnerable to the criticism that his decisions were influenced by his political associations. In fact, there are other aspects of the monarch's service to the nation which are of almost equal benefit to the community, though less dramatic than participation in constitutional crises. One aspect of this work is the frequent appearance of the Queen among her subjects visiting hospitals, schools, exhibitions, factories, scientific establishments, the Armed Forces, and the great occasions of sport. This has double value. It suggests a complete fusion of interest between the Queen and those who are working in a great variety of occupations. Secondly, in spite of the superficial cynicism which many affect, it is a stimulus towards high achievement for any group of people to discover that their activities are sufficiently valuable to the nation to justify a visit from the monarch. It is true that this function could also be performed by a President, but the continuity of the British monarchy makes it unique among the nations of Europe, and earns for it a special respect; immunity from invasion and from destructive revolution has made it easier and more attractive to preserve in Britain our contacts with the past; the monarchy is an outstanding example. It would be a radical break with the past to replace monarchy with a Presidential system of government. Moreover, while it is true that a President could perform the social duties of the monarch with almost equal effectiveness, and without the suggestion of the existence of a social hierarchy implicit in the British concept of monarchy, the political impartiality of the monarchy gives that institution a clear advantage over a Presidential system, both in the occasional exercise of the prerogative powers and, in addition, in the unique role which the monarch holds in relation to the Commonwealth.

The relationship of the monarch to the members of the Commonwealth makes her almost irreplaceable. Loyalty to an abstract conception of Commonwealth unity is remotely feasible, but the ability of the Queen by her visits to personify the conception is a far more effective and satisfying reminder of the links between member countries than any other solution which could be devised. A President has party associations as well as being the representative of the nation. He will represent much to which party politicians and other members of the Commonwealth communities will have the strongest objections. Against the Queen, remote from political controversy, similar objections could not be raised. Moreover, monarchy is an institution embedded in the history of many of the African members of the Commonwealth in particular. For them identification of loyalty to the Commonwealth and personal loyalty to the Queen is an easy matter. This direct relationship does not apply among all the member countries. In recent times, Ghana, India, and Pakistan, for instance, have become Republics, for whom the monarch is not personally a ruler, in the sense that she is Queen of Canada, or Queen of Australia; for the Republican members the monarch is merely a symbol of Commonwealth unity, and her leadership is only accepted in that sense. This does not mar the personal relationship between the monarch and the Republican countries which she visits, as her tours of India and Ghana have shown in recent times. Nor is there any lack of enthusiasm for the monarchy in egalitarian countries such as Australia, where social divisions are less solidly stratified than they are in Britain. It is true that self-interest economically, politically, and strategically, must be one of the strongest bonds in maintaining the unity of the Commonwealth when there are so many differences of outlook among the component members, but it is desirable for the reasons previously indicated that there should be a head, even though the leadership is merely a formality, and no other person can fulfil this function so satisfactorily as the monarch.

'The state of the monarchy is the supremest thing upon earth' said James I. His confidence looks strangely archaic now. Yet, shorn of most of its powers, the British monarchy has enough of its ancient vigour left to make it of some value still. Moreover, its essential flexibility has enabled it to adapt itself to the present background of modern democracy without any incongruity, and to change from the direct personal rule of the old Empire to the unique symbolic leadership of the Commonwealth. When the constitutional functions of the monarchy are fully understood, the arguments that the monarchy is an anachronism carry little conviction. Many of the functions performed by the monarchy are useful; some of them are essential, and are far better performed by a non-partisan monarch than by a politician. If, for instance, the monarchy were to be abolished, and the monarch replaced as Head of State by a politician, the political impartiality, which is one of the strongest assets of monarchy in governmental crises, would disappear with that institution itself. Nor would it be at all easy to preserve that dexterous division between power and prestige, which, on the whole, is maintained at the moment.

FURTHER READING

Sir Charles Petrie, *The Modern British Monarchy* (Eyre & Spottiswoode, 1961).
D. Morrah, *The Work of the Queen* (Kimber, 1958).
Sir John Wheeler-Bennett, *King George VI* (Macmillan, 1958).
    See also Comments on Further Reading, p. 165.

2

The Supremacy of the Cabinet

The dominant position of the Cabinet. The need for close scrutiny of the term 'Cabinet'. Cabinet functions. Comparative stability of British Governments. Party discipline. Collective responsibility. Supremacy of Act of Parliament. Factors leading to greater centralisation. The degree of Cabinet freedom over policy-making. Public opinion. The Press. Back-benchers. Pressure-groups. The Opposition. The influence of conventional attitudes on political behaviour.

THEME: Cabinet authority has been greatly extended. Formal limitations to its power are negligible, and, in practice, custom provides the best protection.

The supremacy of the Cabinet in the constitution is now generally accepted. The theory of Parliamentary sovereignty might have been tenable at times in the nineteenth century, when it was possible for Bagehot to regard the Cabinet as merely a committee of Parliament, but it is not held to have much relevance to present-day conditions. In *The British Constitution* Sir Ivor Jennings writes 'No change or development of policy of any importance would be carried out without Cabinet sanction'; and earlier in the same book he writes 'The Cabinet can always have the last word'.[1] Other commentators have come to the same conclusion that it is the Cabinet, not Parliament, which is the driving force behind the machinery of government. That this should be so is one more example of the paradoxes of the British constitution, for the Cabinet, in spite of its importance, is scarcely mentioned at all in statutes. Yet the Cabinet does not possess unbridled power. L. S. Amery in *Thoughts on the Constitution* writes 'In no other country is there such a concentration of power, and such a capacity for decisive action as that possessed by a British Cabinet', but he goes on to say 'provided always that it enjoys the support of a

[1] *Ibid.*, p. 153.

majority in the House of Commons'.[1] If this were so it might be arguable that Parliamentary sovereignty is not so moribund an idea as it is sometimes thought to be. In fact, as will be seen later, the influence of the House of Commons over the Cabinet falls far short of sovereignty, though not to the level of being entirely negligible. The dominance of the Cabinet will emerge more clearly from a study of its functions, but it may be of value at the outset to point out that the degree of Cabinet supremacy is apt to elude even the most expert analysis. The supremacy of the Cabinet is not that of an Augustus, nor a Robespierre. It is far more subtle; it relies on co-operation, not coercion, and is itself subject to pressures both from within its own ranks and from outside.

To isolate and describe all the influences which lead to policy decisions is a task which has not been fully attempted yet, nor is it likely that such an analysis will ever be successful when it is made by those whose knowledge is theoretical. The secrecy of Cabinet proceedings establishes a barrier which can be penetrated here and there by intelligent speculation, based on constitutional knowledge, but the man with authoritative knowledge of the influences which shape Cabinet decisions is the Prime Minister. Nor is it likely that these influences will be constant. Prime Ministers and their Cabinets will take more or less account of special interest groups — trade unions, business interests, party groups, and the rest — and of personal and professional advisers according to personal outlook. These matters are apt to be assumed without being explicitly stated in speaking of the constitutional position of the Cabinet. This begins as a matter of convenience since it is easier for frequent reference to speak of 'the Cabinet' than of the variously composed specialist groups whose influence on policy-making is probably greater than that of the Cabinet as a whole. Yet there is a danger in using the term 'Cabinet' indiscriminately if it creates the impression of policy decisions being evolved by the Cabinet of some twenty ministers acting as a single unit. This point has been clearly made in *The British Cabinet* by J. P. Mackintosh. He shows that most of the functions which are normally described as being performed by the Cabinet are in practice performed by smaller groups of powerful Ministers and professional advisers under the central direction of the Prime Minister. This is necessary partly because of the unwieldy size of the Cabinet, and partly

[1] *Ibid.*, p. 70.

because of the highly specialised knowledge which is required if discussions are to have any value. It may well be desirable, for instance, to include a Minister of Transport in any modern Cabinet, but it would be surprising if he had any original contribution to make on matters outside his immediate sphere, such as colonial affairs or trade agreements. Mackintosh goes so far as to say that the formation of policy is not primarily a matter for the Cabinet at all. 'Decisions are made in the departments, in Cabinet Committees, in private talks between the Prime Minister and the Ministers mainly concerned, and the differences that remain are settled in the Cabinet itself.' He goes on to say that 'The main task of the Cabinet is to co-ordinate the work of the various departments and committees, and thus ensure that the activity of the government has a certain coherence'.[1] This view is valuable in removing the ambiguity resulting from the use of the term 'Cabinet' as if it performed the functions of government as a single entity. This does not mean, however, that the Cabinet is merely a channel through which policy decisions flow. While it is true that most of the Cabinet Ministers will be specialists in relatively narrow sectors of policy, all of them are politicians. They are fully entitled, therefore, to oppose a decision because of its possible political repercussions; and, in this respect, the fact that they lack the expert knowledge to formulate the policy or to criticise it in detail is of no consequence whatsoever.

Even on this basis alone, therefore, the Cabinet as a single unit is still in a position of outstanding importance in the constitution; and if one uses the word 'Cabinet' as an umbrella term to comprise the activities of the policy-making groups previously described, the statements made about the dominance of the Cabinet are fully justified, as is evident from any formal statement of its functions. Using the term 'Cabinet' in the sense just described it can be said that the Cabinet initiates most legislation, controls the timing of its entry into Parliament through the advice of its Legislation Committee, and safeguards its passage through its Parliamentary stages by the exercise, when necessary, of the powers of party discipline. The Queen's Speech at the beginning of each Parliamentary session is, in fact, a statement of the programme of the Government, and is prepared by the leading Ministers of the Cabinet. The Cabinet controls all executive activities of central Government. It

[1] J. P. Mackintosh, *The British Cabinet*, p. 382.

reorganises Departments, as the War Office was reorganised in 1904, for instance; it sets up new Ministries, such as the Ministry of Pensions and National Insurance; it settles disputes between Departments; it secures co-ordination by ensuring that Government Departments work towards a common purpose, such as reduction in expenditure, or by mutual consultation and the circulation of information, so that no one Department takes action prejudicial to another simply through a failure of liaison. The Cabinet examines all major issues of foreign and domestic policy: the Berlin situation, our policy at the United Nations, the European Common Market, the attainment of Commonwealth status by dependent territories, the pay pause, the defence of Kuwait, emergency arrangements in the event of transport strikes, these and a host of other matters are not merely subjects for discussion, but also at times for urgent decision. The only exception of any real consequence to this constant review of matters of high policy is the Budget, since it is desirable that the detailed terms should be known to as few as possible before its 'opening' in the House of Commons.

In addition, the Cabinet through its various committees is responsible for the specialised examination and planning of major aspects of Government work. Details of these Cabinet Committees are not disclosed until after the lifetime of the Government concerned. This is the standard practice with both parties and is due not to any reprehensible obsession with secrecy, but to the wish to leave chairmen of Committees and members free from the influence of public and political pressure groups while the necessary researches and negotiations are put into effect. This does not by-pass criticism since ultimately the work of the Committees must be submitted to the Cabinet, and then, if approved, to Parliament. This valuable preliminary planning cannot be carried out in an atmosphere of heated controversy, though the Government will have to face this later when the proposals are scrutinised in Parliament in the form of legislation or policy. There is, therefore, nothing sinister in the secrecy associated with Cabinet Committee proceedings. It is true, nevertheless, that planning the development of the main aspects of government, which is the direct responsibility of the Cabinet, is a far-reaching power, even though it does not involve in Britain conscription and direction of labour, as it does, and has done, elsewhere. Although details of the committees of the present Government are not available, Lord Morrison in *Government and Parliament* has described very fully the committees used by the 1945–51 Labour Governments.[1] A few of these, such as the Reconstruction Committee, will have lost their relevance now, but many of the others were dealing with recurrent issues and are likely to have survived in the organisation of later Governments. The names alone of the most important committees, and there are thirty in all mentioned by Lord Morrison as being in existence at different times in this post-war period, give some insight into the range of subjects examined by Cabinet Committees, and from this their extensive influence can be deduced. Because of their extreme importance there must be a Defence Committee and an Economic Policy Committee. Because of post-war developments and the nature of the issues involved, a Cabinet Committee on Commonwealth Affairs would be as appropriate now as it was in Mr. Attlee's Government, when he himself presided over it. The frequency with which the Prime Minister appeared as chairman of Cabinet Committees — he was chairman of seven in the 1945–51 Labour Governments — is in itself some indication of their importance. There will naturally be a Legislation Committee to assist in working out the priority of the various legislative proposals to be brought before Parliament. Amongst many other committees Lord Morrison also mentions committees for specific areas, such as the Far East and Middle East Committees, committees on economic matters, such as committees for Production, and for Distribution and Marketing, and committees for social services, such as Housing and the National Health Service.

This examination of the functions of the Cabinet gives some indication of its dominance. Apart from the work it does, however, there are political and constitutional factors which give it a stability not enjoyed, for instance, by French Cabinets in recent years. The expectation, based on history, that British Governments of the twentieth century are far more likely than not to last for a period of four or five years is a factor in this stability. At the end of the five years an election becomes statutory, and only the occurrence of war or some other great emergency would render this inoperative. Sometimes a Prime Minister will seek a dissolution after four years of power, as Mr. Macmillan did in 1959, not because a dissolution was forced upon him by the weakness of his Government, but

[1] *Ibid.*, pp. 16–27.

c

because the moment seemed opportune. This is a perfectly legitimate political device towards the end of a Government's period of power. Dissolutions after a shorter period of power would in normal circumstances be regarded with some suspicion, so that it is a fair assumption that a party with a sound working majority will stay in power for four or five years, with all the advantages involved of continuity of policy over that period. Where there have been exceptions in this century they have been due mostly to situations created by election results unlikely to occur very commonly. The Labour Governments of 1924 and 1929–31, for instance, had no absolute majority, and were therefore dependent on Liberal support, a weakening factor. The 1950–1 Labour Government had such a slender majority that Mr. Attlee, to avoid the physical and mental strain involved for his supporters in the constant need to use the votes of every Labour M.P. on every major occasion, asked for a dissolution; the financial crisis of 1951 intensified the difficulties of a struggling government. The Conservatives, too, have experienced brief sessions of power, as when Mr. Baldwin in 1923, after a few months, appealed to the voters for their views on Protection.

These incidents, however, involved rather special circumstances, and there is no intrinsic reason why a Government with a working majority should expect anything less than four years of power. The basis of that power is the will of the electors expressed through their votes. After that initial stage has been reached, and the victorious party has formed a Government, a new element comes into play, the power of party discipline. Party discipline is not enforced with mechanical rigidity. It is obvious that not all M.P.s in the Government party will have identical views on all issues. The post-war Parliaments alone give ample evidence of these differences of opinion within the parties. Peter Richards, analysing these incidents in *Honourable Members*, points out that there were nine major Labour 'rebellions' during the 1945–51 Government; nor is the Conservative record very different.[1] 'Rebellion' may be a more dramatic word than the circumstances justify but it is clear that total obedience in all circumstances is fortunately still beyond the bounds of present possibility. It needs to be remembered also that if even a small number of Government supporters vote against their party, or abstain, the element of

[1] *Ibid.*, pp. 148–53.

doubt created over the wisdom of Government policies is magnified out of all proportion to the numbers involved, with consequent damage to electoral prospects. Admittedly this might be interpreted as an argument for greater coercion of M.P.s by the Whips. In practice, uniformity of approach cannot be secured by disciplinary measures alone in the parties as they are constituted at present. The risk of losing the support of members remains a deterrent against the adoption of controversial measures in spite of the prevalence of the Gilbertian belief that M.P.s vote 'just as their leaders tell them to'. Apart from the not infrequent crises within the parties, such as that created within the Conservative Party in 1954 when twenty-eight of its members forming the 'Suez Group' opposed concessions to Nasser, instances of small-scale opposition to Government actions by its supporters are fairly commonplace. In February, 1962, for instance, three Conservative M.P.s voted against the scheme for the reorganisation of Greater London. In May, 1963, fifteen Conservative M.P.s either abstained or voted against the Government decision to deport Chief Enahoro to Nigeria. Defections of this kind are not followed by the immediate retribution of the withdrawal of the whip. For the Conservative Party particularly, if any penalty at all is incurred it is more likely to be the penalty of not being re-adopted for the next election rather than expulsion from the Parliamentary party. These facts lend some support to the belief that party discipline is neither so rigid nor so intolerant of individual differences as is sometimes alleged. Even when the Chief Whip interviews M.P.s hostile to some aspect of Government policy his primary purpose is persuasion rather than coercion.

Any assessment of the leader-member relationship within the parties should take into account the existence of the Parliamentary Labour Party, and also of the 1922 Committee for the Conservative Party. These private party meetings of M.P.s give an excellent opportunity for the thrashing out of differences without the restraints imposed when the parties are engaged in the widely publicised activities of the House of Commons. There are differences in their organisation. The Conservative leader and his ministers, for instance, do not normally attend meetings of the 1922 Committee, but the leader is kept informed of the views of members. Contact between the Labour leader and the Parliamentary Labour Party is closer, especially when the Labour Party forms the Opposition. Differences between the two organisations matter less, however, than their similarities. The central purpose for each organisation is to ensure that liaison is maintained between the leadership and members so that all are well informed on the mood and objectives of their respective parties. This gives opportunities for the removal of causes of discord before the issues are brought to public attention. It is a further advantage in securing genuine unity of feeling within the party that ministers have themselves been back-benchers, and may become so again. The precariousness of political office is thus, in itself, an incentive towards good relations between the leadership and members.

When all these necessary reservations have been made it is still true that party discipline is a support for the power of the Cabinet. When there is a sufficient margin of support for the Government to ensure that there is no danger of its defeat it is reasonable for Government M.P.s to make their protest against legislation they dislike, in the hope that this action will bring forcibly to the Government's notice the need for some modification of the bill. There is a consoling factor for British Governments in that, while Government supporters may voice their protests against particular features of Government policy, their dislike for these measures falls far short of their dislike for the policy of the Opposition. The convention by which if a Government is defeated on a major issue of policy it then resigns is a great source of strength to the Cabinet. Most back-benchers would be content to stomach certain unpalatable features of Government policy rather than bring about the downfall of their own leadership. For some it may be a personal factor which influences their outlook. A dissolution of Parliament means a new General Election and the attendant risk of losing one's seat in the House of Commons for a period of four to five years. For the ambitious politician, and for the man who has no satisfactory alternative to a political career, fighting a General Election is not always a hazard which he would willingly bring upon himself before he is obliged to do so. For others the ability of their party to continue as the Government for the full term of office is, ultimately, of more importance than differences over individual acts of policy. Thus it may come about that a member is hostile to a Government measure, but will still vote for it rather than run the risk of shattering party unity. It would be wrong to infer that strong individual feelings are always repressed when party unity is at stake; there are matters of principle involved in individual governmental acts where it may be impossible for an M.P. to continue to give support to the Government. British policy towards Nasser's Egypt is a good recent example, and in pre-war days there was a powerful section of the Conservative Party which opposed the Government policy of self-government for India. But these situations are exceptional. The great bulk of Government legislation and policy receives support which can be counted on with complete assurance, especially if there is the slightest risk of a Government defeat. Obviously this is a source of great confidence to the Cabinet. The stability of government which results is, in general, desirable, but there has been increasing disquiet in post-war years over Cabinet dominance of the party system. Whenever allegations are made that the Executive has become over-powerful in the modern constitution the influence of party discipline will almost certainly be a central point of the argument. How strong that influence is can, perhaps, be assessed from the foregoing remarks.

Just as the maintenance of party unity involves the exercise of some degree of party discipline, so, too, Cabinet unity is maintained by the doctrine of collective responsibility. Individual criticisms of Government policy will be made in the privacy of Cabinet meetings, but everyone concerned is thoroughly aware of the dangers of exposing differences within the Cabinet during Parliamentary debates. A Cabinet split will almost inevitably lead to a party split, and a divided party cannot govern. The rift in the Balfour Government of 1902–5 over the question of the adoption of Protection is a clear illustration of this. Decisions made by the Cabinet require the support of all the Ministers. Individual Cabinet Ministers who have doubts about the wisdom of particular actions have the choice of overcoming their objections or of resigning. On matters of strongly held principle the latter course is the only one. Thus Lord Snowden and Sir Herbert Samuel resigned in 1932 from the National Government because of differences over the economic policy of the Cabinet, and Mr. Bevan resigned from the Labour Government in 1951 through disagreement over defence policy. These were fundamental issues where it would have been impossible for these Ministers to give even passive acquiescence to the policies proposed. Objections on less fundamental differences can be reconciled by Ministers who value party unity highly, and the working of this doctrine is a further source of strength in Cabinet Government. Both this doctrine and the sanction of party discipline have gained in force in this century from the realisation that in Britain there has almost always been a numerous Opposition party, ready instantly to take the place of a wavering Government.

Cabinet dominance is further encouraged by the omnipotence in Britain of Acts of Parliament which can do everything 'but make a man into a woman and a woman into a man'.[1] The Judiciary has no power to refuse to put into operation any law which has been approved by Parliament, however repugnant the measure may seem to a judge's concept of justice. Nor is there a written constitution in Britain, as there is in the United States and elsewhere, laying down fundamental principles which the Executive and Legislature may not infringe. Constitutionally, there are no permanent guarantees of individual freedoms. Magna Charta, Habeas Corpus, the Ballot and Representation of the People Acts could be swept out of existence by Act of Parliament. The abolition of Habeas Corpus followed by the arrest of members of the Opposition would not be constitutionally impossible. The absurdity of the idea suggests that there are other restraints, and these will be considered later, but the fact that Acts of Parliament are now, in practice, an expression of the policy of the Cabinet does mean that there is no formal, impassable barrier to the establishment of an autocratic authority in Britain. Many reasons make such an action wildly improbable, but the knowledge of this potentially ultimate authority does strengthen the position of the Cabinet in putting into practice authoritarian policies of a milder nature. The controls imposed by the Labour Government of 1945–51 give some indication of the stringency of direction possible even in peacetime.

The tendency towards authoritarian policies is reinforced by the emergence of new political concepts in modern times. The extension of the franchise in the nineteenth century meant that the main parties acquired a direct interest in the welfare of the working class, and from that time 'laissez-faire' became an outmoded doctrine. The growth of State welfare schemes, of the concept of equality of opportunity, and the increasing need for planned development of the means of transport, and of public services, such as electricity, have meant that it has become commonplace nowa-

---

[1] Though, legally, there is no bar to this either!

days to accept directions from the Executive over issues which simply did not arise in Victorian times. This not only gives the Cabinet more influence over the individual citizen through legislation closely scrutinised in the Houses of Parliament, but also, because of the pressure of time and the complexity of the issues, leads to the increasing influence of instruments of the Executive not directly controlled by Parliament. Special interest groups and expert opinion will often need to be consulted before legislation reaches Parliament, where the increasing volume of legislation makes detailed examination of all issues impossible. Once the Act is passed, the Statutory Instruments — the regulations necessary to make the Act sufficiently detailed to work in practice — are devised by Civil Servants in the Government Departments. Provision is made in Parliamentary procedure for the examination of these regulations to some extent by the whole House of Commons, and also by Select Committees of the Lords and Commons. The sheer volume of regulations makes it physically impossible to scrutinise in detail every Statutory Instrument. In effect, the power of regulation-making has to be delegated to the Civil Servants in the Government Departments, though under general Parliamentary control. It does mean, however, that the normal process by which the Legislature can cushion the general public against unwise decisions by the Executive is not so fully applicable to this kind of legislation. The scope of this legislation is, of course, limited, since the regulations cannot exceed the powers given by the original statute, but it is not always possible to anticipate the full effects of the statutory regulations from the form of the original Statute itself. This is, therefore, another instance of the way the power of the Executive has increased in modern times.

Pressure of time has also meant the development in Parliament of various devices for shortening debate. There is the 'Closure' motion 'that the question be now put'; if a hundred members support it, this has the effect of bringing the debate to an end. There is also the 'Guillotine' procedure, by which the Government can allocate definite times for the completion of the necessary stages of Parliamentary bills, and the 'Kangaroo' procedure which is used in committees, so that the chairman of a Standing Committee can choose the most important amendments for discussion and omit the others. Shortening of debate and of the examination of bills involves obvious dangers since these devices could be exploited by a Government with autocratic tendencies. They are, however, a necessary feature of the political scene when shortage of time handicaps Government legislation, nor is there any great reason to believe that these devices have been abused in recent times.

There is strong evidence to show, therefore, that changing political circumstances in modern Britain have made it more likely that a strong Executive will emerge. So far as this has happened, however, it is due to a change in circumstances and not to any intrinsic change in the outlook of the members of the Cabinet itself. Additional powers are now required, but they are used, in general, with discretion, and with the realisation that the Cabinet is answerable to Parliament, and, ultimately, to the electorate itself. Considering the rapid changes there have been on the Continent in this century, with the emergence of totalitarian governments and of Executives of very great power, and considering also the comparative decline of Legislatures — for Parliamentary Government in the nineteenth century used to be looked on as the apex of political achievement — it is a notable fact that the Cabinet is still believed to be more akin to a representative institution than would be possible in a dictatorship. If it seems at times to be autocratic in its behaviour, it is an autocracy not welcomed, but an involuntary 'dictatorship' forced on the Cabinet by pressure of time and circumstance. It is always possible for critics to infer more sinister motives, but the limits which all Governments must impose on the absolute freedom of citizens if they are to govern at all are more elastic in Britain than those which exist in the governmental systems of many other major powers.

There is no doubt, however, that, even in Britain, individual and group freedoms are less solidly based than they used to be. In view of this increasing challenge to what have generally been regarded as fundamental rights, it would be of interest to examine the limitations on the power of the Cabinet. If the final test of authority in the State lies in the power of dismissal of other institutions of government, who possesses this ultimate authority in Britain? It is clearly no longer the monarch. Edward VIII's abdication showed that if there was a divergence of opinion between the monarch and a Government, acting in the name of a duly elected House of Commons, it must be the monarch who gives way. The Cabinet has claims to supreme authority in that it can dismiss Parliament if the Prime Minister asks for a dissolution. It is also true that Parliament can dismiss the Cabinet by passing a vote of no confidence. Whichever takes place the matter does not end there. In dismissing Parliament the Cabinet is dismissing itself and a General Election becomes necessary. If, on the other hand, Parliament dismisses the Government by giving majority support to a vote of no confidence, that does not involve an immediate election since a Government can be formed from the victorious party. It has been the practice, however, except when wartime exigencies make it impossible, to follow up a Government defeat of this kind with an election very shortly afterwards. Government resignations in 1905, and 1922, for instance, were followed very rapidly by General Elections. This suggests that the final authority in the constitution resides not in Parliament, nor in the Cabinet, but in the electorate itself. Yet this opinion needs to be scrutinised more closely before it is accepted.

It is undoubtedly true that the British live in a sufficiently free society to be able to make the Government fully aware of the state of opinion in a variety of ways. What is much less certain is the degree to which Governments are influenced by public opinion. Newspapers are sometimes considered to be representative of public opinion though in fact the opinions they express may simply be those of their editors and proprietors and are not necessarily representative even of their own particular readers. Their influence on policy-making is normally negligible. Where they can be valuable is in their exposure of any obvious abuse of power by politicians or civil servants. Respect for the individual freedoms is still well established in Britain, though less so in modern times. It is still easy for the Press to rouse public sympathy for hardship imposed by intolerant treatment of individuals. This is a different matter from the forming of policy, however, and in policy-making it appears that the influence of the Press and of public opinion is of little account. As an example, a Government which was entirely responsive to public opinion would be far more hesitant than it has been in its intention to take Britain into the European Common Market. Governments are expected to provide leadership. This they can hardly do by consulting newspapers and public opinion polls before they act. Public reaction to policies after they are formed may, on the other hand, be a matter of close interest to Governments since unfavourable reactions can obviously mar a party's electoral prospects. Even in this respect Governments can afford to remain unmoved in their policies for much of the time since the modern public is apt to lose all critical sense in the volume of news with which it is deluged, and its memory is notoriously short. The Conservative Party was able to re-establish itself sufficiently to win the 1959 election in spite of the vehement criticism of the Suez Canal expedition in 1956. In the last months of office the Government will be anxious to make a favourable impression upon voters, but there is no reason to suppose that the influence of the general public is of great consequence otherwise.

It could perhaps be claimed that the back-benchers represent another way of bringing pressure to bear on Cabinet policies on behalf of the general public. The extent to which back-bencher opinion is influenced by opinion in constituencies is one of the many imponderables in politics. It is clear, however, that Cabinet policies cannot be put into effect without reference to the opinion of Government back-benchers, conveyed to the Party leaders by means of private meetings or by the Party Whips. The views of functional committees of Government back-benchers, for instance, deserve particular respect. The support of the party's back-benchers must obviously be retained if a Government is to survive. This is not generally difficult since both the Cabinet and the back-benchers are strongly bound together by the belief that, whatever their differences in detail, their own continuance in office is of greater importance still. Governmental splits have broken up ministries, but there have been no instances of this happening since 1945, so that the threat of the withdrawal of back-bencher support is not likely to be felt acutely by Cabinets. The chief value of back-bencher opinion is that it acts as a pressure-gauge of party feeling. This opinion does not influence the activity of the Cabinet very much so long as the reading is normal, but is a valuable instrument for indicating when an explosion is about to take place.

Special interest groups such as Trade Unions, employers' organisations, and City interests, are in a stronger position for modifying the formation of Cabinet policy, since their specialist knowledge places them upon a nearer equality with the expert advisers who formulate policy under the direction of the Prime Minister, and to some extent of the whole Cabinet. Apart from that, the powerful interests represented by these pressure-groups make their co-operation desirable. Yet it is absurd to visualise government being carried on as a kind of conspiracy against the nation with the Prime Minister and Cabinet giving a frontage of constitutional respectability to the machinations of shadowy figures representative of Big Business, Trade Unions, or some other favourite aversion. Pressure-groups represent special interests; as a result their view of politics is both narrow and vulnerable. The Prime Minister and his chief ministers, with their wider view of politics, can sometimes, for instance, rely on opposing influences to cancel each other out, as the left wing of the Labour Party and the Trade Union leaders are apt to do. Sometimes a Government can show that in the interests of wider national progress the special interests of a pressure-group may have to be overridden. This is a critical test of the extent of Government authority over the powerful special interest groups. An example of this situation occurred in 1962 in the negotiations between the railwaymen's unions and the British Transport Commission over the latter's decision to reduce railway staffs in the interests of economy. Even though the large Trade Unions are extremely powerful, there has been no indication in this episode, and little indication in previous ones, that Governments can be coerced into modifying an unpopular policy. The Government always has the advantage in dealing with these pressure-groups that it can legitimately claim that the whole is more important than the parts, that national interests matter more than sectional interests, and that even the most powerful of the pressure-groups only represent a minority of voters.[1]

A further restraint to be considered on the dominance of the Cabinet is the existence of an Opposition capable of forming an alternative Government. Far from Opposition being regarded as iniquitous, or even treasonable, as it has been elsewhere, the leader is given the title of Leader of Her Majesty's Opposition, and is paid a salary of £3,000 a year to emphasise the importance attached to criticism of Government policy. A strong Opposition can, when thoroughly organised, bring intensive scrutiny to bear on Government policy. Its criticisms receive a very wide circulation through the Press, television, and radio, and this helps to produce an atmo-

[1] The recently created National Economic Development Council, however, with members drawn from the T.U.C. and from employers, is so broadly based that potentially it could be regarded as a pressure-group of unusual power.

sphere of opinion to which the Government cannot be entirely indifferent. But, as previously indicated, it is unwise to stress very strongly the influence of public opinion upon Government policies. It is fair to point out also that considering the pressure of Parliamentary business the Opposition is quite well served in the time allotted to it. Apart from the twenty-six Supply Days the Opposition has further opportunities for criticism in the debate on the Queen's Speech, in the debate on the adjournment, in committees, and in motions[1] and questions. It may even happen, as it did with the Labour Governments of 1945–51 on the issue of nationalised industries, that the Government will itself allocate additional time to the Opposition for debates. Yet, in practice, there is very little relationship between the volume of criticism made and the amount of change effected. A Government with a safe majority can afford to ignore the advice of political opponents. It is in the meetings of the Standing Committees to examine the details of legislation rather than in the more spectacular setting of the House of Commons debates that the Opposition can most effectively bring some influence to bear on Government policy.

The view that the authority of the Cabinet can be tempered by public opinion is broadly true in that there are many ways in which the opinions of the general public and of particular sections of it can be expressed. But it should be clear from the foregoing remarks that the Cabinet is not under any irresistible pressure from any quarter in its policy-making. A determined Government can override the objections of even the strongest pressure-group so long as it can count on the support of its own party. It may even pursue a policy to which a minority of the party has strong objections provided again that an essential nucleus of support remains. This has been demonstrated since the war both in the ministries of Mr. Attlee when sections of the Labour Party opposed his defence policy, and in the ministry of Mr. Macmillan when there have been divergences over financial and economic policy. It may seem, therefore, that a Cabinet differs very little from more specifically authoritarian Governments. Yet it should be remembered that there are restraints on the Cabinet less tangible than those so far described, but more effective. These are the restraints which spring from the habitual attitudes of governors and governed, from

---

[1] An official Opposition motion of censure must be debated, by Parliamentary convention, within a few days of its appearance on the paper.

convention, from tacit assumptions on what constitutes a reasonable degree of Government control over the activities of the people it rules. These are the real limitations on Cabinet authority. Their effectiveness will last as long as public opinion is sufficiently educated to recognise them. It is obvious, however, that limitations of this type lack the precision of legal definition. The Cabinet, using that term to comprise the various informed groups who devise policy, has sufficiently wide powers over a great range of activities to justify the claim that it is supreme in the constitution.

FURTHER READING

J. P. Mackintosh, *The British Cabinet* (Stevens, 1962).

Sir Ivor Jennings, *Cabinet Government* (C.U.P., 3rd Edition, 1959).

Lord Morrison, *Government and Parliament* (O.U.P., 3rd Edition, 1964).

Lord Campion (Ed.), *British Government Since 1918* (Allen & Unwin, 1950).

Lord Campion (Ed.), *Parliament — A Survey* (Allen & Unwin, 1963).

J. D. Stewart, *British Pressure Groups* (O.U.P., 1958).

R. T. McKenzie, *British Political Parties* (Heinemann, 2nd Edition, 1963).

See also Comments on Further Reading, p. 165.

3

Prime Minister and Cabinet

Membership of the Cabinet. The responsibilities of the Prime
Minister. The choice of Ministers. Organisation of duties. The
relationship of the Prime Minister to the Cabinet, the Crown,
Parliament, his party, the Civil Service, and to the community.
The burden of Ministerial work. The idea of a small Cabinet.

THEME: The pressure of governmental work in modern times;
its influence on the Prime Minister's position and on Cabinet
organisation.

The number of Ministerial posts has risen remarkably since
the First World War. Including the Ministers of State,
Under-Secretaries, Parliamentary Secretaries, and other
lesser posts the total is little short of one hundred. The holders of
these offices are nominated by the Prime Minister, who also
nominates the Cabinet. There will normally be some twenty members in the Cabinet, though in war-time urgency of decision makes
necessary a smaller number. Winston Churchill's war Cabinet
consisted of a maximum number of nine members, for instance. In
peace-time the size of the Cabinet has usually varied little during
the century. Lord Salisbury's Government at the beginning of the
century had a Cabinet of twenty as did Mr. Attlee's Government
at first in 1945. This tendency for most Prime Ministers to appoint
Cabinets of virtually the same size suggests that there are certain
basic considerations to be observed irrespective of the differing
qualities of individual Prime Ministers.

From closer examination of the membership of the Cabinet it is
apparent that certain Ministers will inevitably be included because
of the importance of their office. The Foreign Secretary, Home
Secretary, the Chancellor of the Exchequer, and the Lord Chancellor are all, almost *ex officio*, members of the Cabinet. Some
Ministers will be members because of their representative capacity.

The Secretaries of State for Scotland, Commonwealth Relations, and the Colonies, come into this category which can almost be defined as geographical representation.[1] A few members, the Lord President of the Council, the Lord Privy Seal and, often, the Chancellor of the Duchy of Lancaster, will be included, not because of the importance of their formal duties in connection with these posts, for they are almost nominal, but to allow some flexibility in the performance of new functions. Mr. Macleod, for instance, has combined the office of Chancellor of the Duchy of Lancaster with that of Leader of the House. These 'spare' Ministers are also useful for their ability to act as chairmen of Cabinet Committees. The Lord President of the Council was chairman of the Cabinet Committee examining the plans for the nationalisation of industries in the post-war Labour Government, and led several other Cabinet Committees too. The additional freedom of the non-departmental Ministers also enables them to lead important delegations. Mr. Heath, the Lord Privy Seal, has fulfilled this role in respect of the European Common Market negotiations. The remaining places in the Cabinet are filled partly by reference to the function performed; thus the Minister for Defence (especially since the recent reorganisation), the Minister for Housing and Local Government, and the President of the Board of Trade will certainly be included. Other leading Ministers are less assured of Cabinet rank. The Minister of Education, for instance, was excluded in 1950. But, in addition, the Prime Minister will choose members for personal reasons. The doctrine of collective responsibility means that there must be a strong sense of unity among Cabinet members, and some readiness to compromise is a desirable qualification. The Prime Minister must be guided in his choice, therefore, by his assessment of the willingness, or otherwise, of colleagues to recognise that extremes of individualism are as undesirable as extremes of loyalty.

Amongst all the Ministers of the Crown the Prime Minister, as his title suggests, is pre-eminent. He has been described as 'the first among equals' to stress the democratic nature of his position, but an examination of his responsibilities suggests that this is an underestimate, and that his powers between elections are very great indeed, stronger, for instance, than those of a President of the

[1] In July, 1962, the posts of Secretary of State for the Colonies and of Secretary of State for Commonwealth Relations were combined.

United States. One of his duties is already plain from a study of the way in which the Cabinet is composed. The choice of Ministers is essentially his own. There may be pressure for the inclusion of certain outstanding personalities amongst his colleagues, and he may yield to this pressure, but only if he is satisfied that his action will in no way weaken his own leadership or endanger Cabinet unity. These are the primary considerations which will influence his choice, and the popularity of possible Cabinet Ministers is only one factor in his decision. It may even be that he will offer a Cabinet post to someone who is not a Minister, or even an M.P. Balfour, in 1903, offered the post of Colonial Secretary to Lord Milner on the resignation of Joseph Chamberlain, though Milner had never played any active part in Parliamentary life. There have been several instances since. This practice illustrates the freedom of choice of the Prime Minister in a vital function of government.

Having chosen the Cabinet the Prime Minister must allocate the duties according to his judgment of the special abilities of the members. He must decide what Cabinet Committees there will be, appoint the Chairmen, preside over some Committees himself — Mr. Attlee was chairman of Committees for Commonwealth Affairs, Far Eastern Affairs, Economic Policy, Housing, National Health Service, Food and Fuel, and Indian Affairs, during his two Ministries, 1945–51 — and keep in touch with the work of the other Cabinet Committees, where he does not preside himself. The importance of the guidance and co-ordination he supplies can be deduced from the vast range of topics discussed at Cabinet Committee meetings. The Prime Minister's central position admirably fits him to give advice to the chairmen of these Committees, and to individual Ministers. He can do so the more effectively since, of modern British leaders, Sir Alec Douglas-Home, Mr. Macmillan, Sir Anthony Eden, Mr. Attlee, and Mr. Churchill, had all had Ministerial experience before they became Prime Ministers. We are never again likely to have a twenty-four-year-old Prime Minister like Pitt, George III's nominee in 1783.

The Prime Minister organises the agenda of Cabinet meetings. He has been greatly helped in recent times by the work of the Cabinet Office. This organisation is valuable not only for its routine office activities and research findings from its statistical and planning sections, but also for the assistance which it can give to the Prime Minister in co-ordinating the activities of the Cabinet,

Cabinet Committees, and sub-committees. These are tasks which would be beyond the power of one man, but which nevertheless need central direction. The Cabinet Office is almost becoming a Prime Minister's Department on its own. In 1962 the post of Secretary to the Cabinet, which had been combined with the function of Head of the Civil Service, became a separate appointment. The salary has been fixed at £500 a year more than that paid to the heads of Government Departments, an indication of its great and growing importance.[1]

The Prime Minister's task of acting as chairman of Cabinet meetings is of crucial importance. He has a heavy responsibility, for it is at these meetings that Government policy must be hammered into shape before it is transmitted to Parliament. The burden becomes additionally great if there are differences of opinion between Ministers at the meeting. The duty of reconciling these differences belongs directly to the Prime Minister; if he fails, he may shatter the Government and the party and leave his leadership self-condemned, as Balfour's was by 1905, though Balfour was working against difficulties which, objectively, invite sympathy. Differences within the Cabinet do not always have this spectacular effect, but the ultimate threat of an overthrow of the Government must always be present as a latent factor in any division of opinion. Prime Ministers, no doubt, are often successful in patching up differences, but the general public hears nothing of disputes successfully settled. Sometimes the dissentient at a Cabinet meeting gains little or no support from his colleagues, and then, if he persists in opposition, the only recourse open to him is resignation. This is less serious from the point of view of maintaining the Government in power, but it will still not be a cause of satisfaction to the Prime Minister who must be conscious at all times of the paramount need to maintain unity of outlook. No one has responsibilities akin to his in this vital respect. He is undoubtedly helped by the convention that votes are not taken at Cabinet meetings; instead, the Prime Minister declares the sense of the meeting, thus giving him more room for manoeuvre.

One of the most significant features which emerges from an

---

[1] See P. Bromhead, 'The British Constitution in 1962', pp. 132–3, in *Parliamentary Affairs*, Spring, 1963. The salary has since been increased to £8,800 (September, 1963), £600 a year more than the new scale for Departmental heads.

D

analysis of the functions of the Prime Minister is that his personal influence is dominant in so many different phases of Government activity. The Queen's prerogative powers, for instance, are now harnessed with rare exceptions to Government policy; conventional constitutional usage and the close relationship which springs up between a monarch and the Prime Minister from their frequent contacts give the Prime Minister considerable influence over the remaining powers of the monarchy. He has the duty of keeping the monarch informed of political developments, and Lord Rosebery, for instance, when he was Prime Minister in 1894, was severely taken to task by Queen Victoria for failing to give her prior notice of the sharp criticisms he made of the House of Lords. The Prime Minister also advises the Crown on the use of the prerogative power of dissolution, and, except in unusual circumstances, this will be his personal decision (see Chapter 1). The prerogative powers of appointment are also exercised on the advice of the Prime Minister. He chooses the Ministers inside the Cabinet and outside. He chooses the Governors of colonies, and can influence strongly the compilation of the Honours List, particularly in the creation of peers. He also appoints bishops, though the advice of the Archbishop of Canterbury should weigh heavily with him here; there is, too, a growing feeling that these episcopal appointments should be made exclusively by the Church itself without reference to lay opinion however distinguished. Apart from the formal relationship to the Crown in the exercise of the various prerogative powers, the Prime Minister will also act as a personal adviser to the monarch, particularly on matters such as the desirability of visits to Commonwealth and foreign countries. The consultations between the Queen and Mr. Macmillan which preceded the royal visit to Ghana in 1961, when there seemed to be an element of personal danger involved for the monarch, are a recent example.

Towards Parliament in general, and towards his own supporters there in particular, the Prime Minister has special responsibilities. The extension of the franchise and the reductions in the powers of the House of Lords have made it virtually certain that nowadays the Prime Minister will be a member of the House of Commons. The last Prime Minister in the House of Lords was Lord Salisbury who resigned in 1902. The extensive duties of the Prime Minister make it unlikely that he will hold the formal office of Leader of the House of Commons, but there will be many occasions during the life of his Ministry when he must be the official spokesman and defender of Government policy. He may have to defend one of his colleagues in difficulty, he may need to rally wavering elements in the party, he may need to take the lead over some vital national issue. These are great responsibilities and failure to inspire confidence in Government policies can only lead to defeat and resignation. Balfour's failure to unite the Conservatives over the Protectionist issue, and Chamberlain's failure to inspire confidence over the Government's measures to meet the German offensives of 1940 are instances. Effective leadership must be based on close contact with party opinion. The aloofness and reserve of Ramsay MacDonald and of Neville Chamberlain, and the indifference of Lloyd George to the need to secure maximum party support, all militated against sound leadership. Ideally the Prime Minister should have a personality which earns him not only the loyalty of his own party but also a measure of grudging respect from the Opposition. If, unlike MacDonald for instance, he takes some pleasure in the hurly-burly of debate, and has a combative nature, his duties in the House of Commons will run the more closely with his inclinations. Apart from these more stirring duties, it is also the responsibility of the Prime Minister to plan Parliamentary business with the Government Chief Whip, whose offices at 12, Downing Street are conveniently close.

Since the Civil Service, in its Administrative Grade particularly, provides the mechanism by which the decisions of the Government in Parliament can be put into effect, the Prime Minister has the ultimate authority for appointments to senior administrative posts. A change in Government means that a new set of personal relationships has to be established between the newly appointed Minister and the leading Civil Servants, such as the Permanent Secretary of his particular Department. The tradition of loyalty to the Minister, and concentration on the means of making a policy workable, irrespective of the worth of the policy itself, makes it improbable that Civil Servants will become at cross-purposes with their Ministers. If this does happen, however, it is undoubtedly the duty of the Prime Minister to resolve the crisis, and he can transfer a Permanent Secretary from one Department to another if he wishes. He will be reluctant to do this since, if it happened very often, it could destroy the goodwill that exists between the Civil Service and the Government. He will also be consulted about all new appointments and has the general responsibility for seeing that Government policy is being put into effect in an efficient and co-ordinated way by the many different Government Departments.

An account of the Prime Minister's duties lends some substance to the allegation that, between elections, his powers differ little from those of a dictator, not perhaps the ideological dictator of modern times, but the 'benevolent despot' of eighteenth-century history with his all-pervasive influence in society. Moreover, the holding of Summit conferences has added to the power of the position. There is, however, a fundamental difference as compared with dictators past and present, and that is in the Prime Minister's relationship to the general public. He must give them guidance and leadership, as Winston Churchill did during the war, or, in a rather different context, as Lord Attlee did in 1948, when he made his successful appeal to the London dockers to end their strike; to that extent there is some kinship between the direct personal impact on the nation exercised by a dictator and that exercised by a Prime Minister: this aspect of his work is, after all, a necessary adjunct of any leadership. The essential difference lies in the idea of account-ability to the nation. Now that television, in particular, has made possible more immediate contact between the Prime Minister and the people, explanation of Government policy through the tele-vising of party political talks, interviews, and great occasions, has become a familiar phenomenon. Consciousness of the need to pro-ject a favourable party image to increase prospects of success in any General Election, coupled with realisation of the value of securing popular support for any major issues of Governmental policy, have combined to make the nation much more conscious of the outlook and policies of the Prime Minister than ever before. In a sense, this has led increasingly to 'the cult of the individual', of which the Communists have been so critical in respect of their own past Governments, but the whole approach and manner of these public appearances in Britain make it plain that the Prime Minister is conscious of his accountability both to his party and to the nation.

It would take too long to analyse the functions of the many other Ministers of the Crown as fully as this. The Prime Minister's duties have merited special attention because of their paramount im-portance, and because of the argument that his powers have become dangerously extensive. His duties certainly require tremendous physical and mental resilience, and the briefest examination of the work of the chief Ministers of the Crown leads to the same conclusion, that the responsibilities of government have become so great that a fundamental reorganisation of duties may well become necessary. Lord Morrison's description in *Government and Parliament* of his daily duties during his extensive experience of Ministerial office gives a good insight into the obligations imposed.[1] The reading of official papers, attendance at the House of Commons, possibly to take a decisive part in proceedings there, directions to departmental officials, conferences, deputations, attendance at official functions, Cabinet meetings, and preparation for the next day's business, make heavy demands on the Minister's energy. Moreover, the weight of work is increased by knowledge of its importance and the far-reaching effects of any wrong decision. Nor is the strain greatly relieved at week-ends since the Minister will often need to attend functions and to deal with constituency problems. Speech-making has become more requisite now with the development of an educated and critical electorate, more avid for news and information than ever before. This burden of work applies to all Ministers but the consensus of opinion is that the duties of the Foreign Secretary, the Chancellor of the Exchequer, the Home Secretary, the Minister for Housing and Local Government, and the President of the Board of Trade, are particularly onerous; so too are those of the Lord President of the Council if he has the co-ordinating duties which Lord Morrison had in the Labour Government. The Ministers of Transport and of Labour may find their duties suddenly extended by the onset of some special emergency such as strike action. There is little doubt that the strain of Ministerial life has shortened the political careers, and even the lives, of some of our post-war leaders. The particular strains of direction of foreign policy, involving the vital issues of war and peace, took their toll on Mr. Ernest Bevin, and later on Sir Anthony Eden (now Lord Avon), and the direction of the nation's economic policy, hampered by the many post-war difficulties, placed great strain on Sir Stafford Cripps in the post-war Labour Government.

Pressure of Ministerial business has led to an examination of possible remedies. The prospects are not very encouraging. The essential consideration is whether there can be any delegation or

[1] *Ibid.*, pp. 60–3.

division of duties. It is difficult to see that there is any possibility of a formal limitation of the functions of the Prime Minister. It is essential that he should be able to intervene, at times, to influence decisions of his Ministers, if only because the nature of his office gives him a deeper sense of national needs than anyone else. He may, therefore, have to overrule a partisan departmental policy from the wider knowledge which he has. His extensive functions prepare him admirably for this essential duty of co-ordination in the national interest. The strain is bound to be great, but he can safeguard himself, as Lord Attlee did, by some measure of delega-tion. Ministers of strong character, in charge of foreign affairs and economic affairs, for instance, can do much to ease the burden on the Prime Minister, and 'spare' Ministers such as the Lord President of the Council can be useful in that they can be made responsible for important sectors of government, possibly involving supervision of two or three individual Ministries. Thus, by wise selection of Ministers and by careful organisation, the Prime Minister can reduce his duties without losing effective control. The increased importance of the Prime Minister's position in this cen-tury has made it unlikely that Premiers will combine with their office that of any other Ministry, as MacDonald was Foreign Secretary, for instance, as well as Prime Minister in the first Labour Government, and as Sir Winston Churchill was Minister of Defence in his 1951 Government.

The idea of a division of duties has led to suggestions for a reorganisation of the Cabinet into two sections, an inner 'planning' Cabinet, and an outer ring of Ministers concerned with day-to-day management of Government Departments. There are several variants of the scheme but the best known is probably that put forward by Mr. Amery in *Thoughts on the Constitution*. He sug-gested that there should be a Cabinet of some half dozen members.[1] These Ministers would be freed of departmental duties. They would deal with current administrative problems by summoning the appropriate departmental Ministers to their meetings, but they would, in addition, have regular meetings to discuss future policy. Both administration and planning would be facilitated by the use of committees. These committees, dealing with matters of immedi-ate urgency, would be presided over by one or other of the super-Ministers. The committees concerned with future policy would be

[1] *Ibid.*, pp. 86–94.

assisted by a research and planning staff. Government policy would be divided into broad groupings such as External Affairs, Economics, and Social Welfare. Over each of these committees a super-Minister would preside unless, as might often happen, the Prime Minister himself attended. The Policy Committees would be responsible for the most effective use of national resources by means of long-term planning.

The plan has much to commend it. One of the main difficulties of Ministers is that it is very easy for them to get so heavily involved in the day-to-day running of their Departments that this factor, coupled with their Parliamentary duties, cramps their outlook, and as one problem presses hard on the heels of another, so it becomes less and less probable that they will be able to take the wider view of policies which would lead to effective long-term planning. Mr. Amery's scheme appears to remove this difficulty, and there would be the added advantage that, with smaller numbers to consult, decisions would be easier. Critics of the scheme are doubtful whether Mr. Amery's claim that there would be no divorce between policy and administration is justified. They feel that the creation of super-Ministers will accentuate a tendency already apparent, to concentrate effective power in the hands of fewer and fewer men. It is feared that these planners, increasingly remote from the realities of personal contact with the problems of day-to-day administration in the Departments, will busy themselves with the production of theoretical reforms of little practical value. Their position of supremacy would lead to a loss of contact with the general state of opinion both in their party and in the country. These criticisms are not entirely convincing. They are based on the assumption, probably false, that these Cabinet Ministers would devise their policies without reference to political realities. There is really no very strong evidence to believe that this is probable. They would be men with practical experience of the Government Departments they were supervising; even if their experience had been of other Government Departments — and this is unlikely — departmental problems have much in common, so that experience of one gives some guidance as to what may happen in another. Moreover, the Prime Minister at the moment performs very much the same functions as these co-ordinating Ministers and this role is not yet regarded as too exacting for one man to perform. The Cabinet Ministers would still be members of

Parliament, they would still represent particular constituencies, and they would still depend for their continuance in office on party support, so that the criticisms made would not appear to have much substance. A criticism with rather more point to it is that the doctrine of accountability of Ministers is harder to apply when there is a supervising Minister as well as an individual Minister in charge of a Government Department. The inconvenience is increased when the supervising Minister is in the House of Lords, and this was a difficulty experienced in Sir Winston Churchill's 1951 Government. There was a small-scale experiment then with the idea of 'overlord' Ministers when Lord Woolton was given control of the Ministries of Agriculture and Food, then separate. Lord Leathers became responsible for the Ministries of Transport, Fuel and Power, and Sir Winston Churchill himself was Minister of Defence as well as Prime Minister. The fact that two of these Ministers were in the House of Lords necessarily made it difficult to allocate responsibility for policy decisions in a way acceptable to the House of Commons, but it is a defect which need not always apply.

Although there are objections to the scheme for a smaller Cabinet, they are not insuperable. It may be that the Cabinet suggested by Mr. Amery is too small in number, but a reduction in numbers along similar lines with some distinction between planning Ministers and those concerned with everyday policy would seem to be worthwhile. There are already signs that changes in this direction are taking place. It has been pointed out previously that the Cabinet is not ideally composed either in numbers or specialised knowledge for detailed policy-making (see Chapter 2). In practice, policy is formulated by consultation between the Prime Minister and a few leading Ministers, supplemented by the advice of Cabinet Committees, and of men with specialist knowledge of the problems involved. Mr. Amery's idea of relieving the 'policy' Ministers of the pressure of departmental business has been partly realised by the appointment of Ministers of State to assist the Ministers in charge of large Government Departments. Two Ministers of State have been appointed, for instance, as deputies to the Foreign Secretary. It is in the major Departments especially that their ability to share the duties of the Minister is of the greatest value in enabling him to stand back a little from the furore of routine business. This is hardly the same as the more thoroughgoing suggestion for reorganisation put forward by Mr. Amery. It would be characteristic of the British approach, though, if reorganisation of the duties of Ministers took place in this piecemeal way rather than in the adoption comprehensively of some new scheme.

FURTHER READING

B. E. Carter, *The Office of Prime Minister* (Faber, 1956).
Sir Ivor Jennings, *Cabinet Government* (C.U.P., 3rd Edition, 1959).
Rt. Hon. L. S. Amery, *Thoughts on the Constitution* (O.U.P., 1953).
Lord Campion (Ed.), *Parliament — a Survey* (Allen & Unwin, 1963).
    See also Comments on Further Reading, p. 165.

4

Ministers and Civil Servants

An assessment of the authority of Civil Servants based on their influence over Parliamentary legislation, their contacts with official organisations, and their influence over administrative decisions. Administrative tribunals. The doctrine of Ministerial Responsibility and its importance.

THEME: Civil Service powers are increasing, but the doctrine of Ministerial Responsibility gives reasonable safeguards for the individual citizen.

In its numbers (over 600,000), in the closeness of association between senior Civil Servants and Ministers, in the extensive and important duties of the Civil Service, and in its permanence (for Governments change, but the Civil Service remains the same), there would seem to be strong reasons for believing that the influence of the Civil Service may be a powerful factor in the formation of Government policy. That Civil Servants are sheltered by anonymity does not make the situation any more reassuring. Nor does the fact that their numbers have increased by over half since pre-war days, partly because of the expansion of work of existing Government Departments, partly because of the creation of new Government Departments. The Ministries of Labour, Transport, Food, Supply, Civil Aviation, National Insurance, Defence, Fuel and Power, and Town and Country Planning, for instance, have all been set up since 1914. In the distant period of the eighteenth century it was considered sufficient at one period to have only two Secretaries of State. Now Government activity has developed so much that it is doubtful whether even the present large number of Government Departments is enough, and from time to time suggestions are made for Ministries of Fine Arts, of Sport, and of Justice.

Pressure of governmental work has led to an increase not only in the number of Civil Servants, but also in their power, since a certain measure of delegation of functions by Parliament to the Civil Service has become essential. Lord Acton's maxim that power tends to corrupt, and its exemplification in the corruption of the Civil Servants in France and Russia in the period preceding their Revolutions in 1789 and 1917, are disquieting reminders of the influence of an over-powerful Civil Service. They are restrained neither from below, since unlike politicians they have no constituents, and have no need to win elections, nor, in the instances quoted, were they restrained from above since the central Governments were little concerned with the implications of their policies in local matters. In more recent times, the German Government in the pre-Nazi period, and the French Government during the Third Republic, had to contend with some measure of opposition from the Civil Service, which obviously involved considerable obstruction in the application of policy. The dangers of a powerful Civil Service are only too apparent. Suggestions that the Civil Service has become too strong in Britain have been made. Lord Hewart's book *The New Despotism* is often quoted as an example of this criticism, and this was published as long ago as 1929. More recently, Civil Service influence on legislation, in the form of Statutory Instruments, and on administrative decisions, in episodes such as the Crichel Down inquiry of 1954, has led to renewed criticisms. It is appropriate, therefore, to examine what opportunities Civil Servants have for influencing governmental policy in Britain.

Legislative activity is primarily a matter for the Government and Parliament, but there are several stages in the process by which a bill becomes an Act where Civil Service influence is felt. There are some types of legislation, concerned with administrative neatness rather than with the initiation of some completely new service, where the senior Civil Servants may quite possibly have a fuller grasp of the requirements than the Minister himself. From their long experience of one particular Department they will have become aware of anomalies in legislation which necessitate the rewording of previous Parliamentary Acts. It may well come about that senior Civil Servants will be the initiators of legislation of this type by suggesting to their Minister the idea of amending legislation. The Minister will become conversant with the range and limits of the changes proposed, but the details of adjustment will largely be left to the Civil Servants themselves. Legislation of this 'tidying-up' kind involves no real risk of abuse of power, and it will have to clear the necessary procedural hurdles in the Houses of Parliament before it is accepted as an Act of Parliament.

A more interesting consideration is the degree of Civil Service influence in general legislation. At whatever level suggestions are put forward involving new legislation on major issues a preliminary committee will have to be appointed with clear terms of reference. Suppose, for instance, that it was suggested that there should be compulsory Civil Defence training for all fit persons between the ages of eighteen and twenty. Since Civil Defence is a Home Office responsibility the Minister would appoint the necessary committee, and, with the help of his senior advisers, would devise specific questions for them to answer. The members of the committee would be drawn largely, possibly exclusively, from his own Department. Detailed plans would involve consultation with a number of Government Departments, the Treasury and the Ministry of Labour being obvious examples in this instance, and the various research and statistical groups might be approached for information on the numbers of people involved in the various areas of the country. Local government authorities would have to be consulted on matters such as the availability of buildings for training centres. The results of the investigations of the committee would then be submitted to the Minister. If he is satisfied with the information given he is then in a position to make a report to the Cabinet, which itself is likely to have been the initiator of an idea as important as this. Up to this stage the work of the Civil Servants, though of value, has clearly been of secondary importance compared with the responsibilities of the Minister and of the Cabinet. The terms of reference for the Committee, and the decision on whether the information given provides a sound basis for legislation are matters which are decided by the politicians. This relationship, with the Civil Service concerned with the provision of information, and the politicians with the responsibility of decision, applies throughout most of the subsequent stages of the bill.

Once the Cabinet has approved the bill in principle, and the Legislation Committee of the Cabinet has decided when the bill is to be fitted into the Parliamentary time-table, the Minister, the departmental Civil Servants, and a Parliamentary counsel, will then spend some considerable time in devising the wording. After several drafts and meetings the bill is then ready for Parliament.

The early stages do not make heavy demands on the Civil Servants. The First Reading is a formality, and before the Second Reading a complete text of the bill must be made available to M.P.s. The Second Reading, the debate on the principles of the bill, can be an exhaustive test of the Minister's grasp of its implications. It would be difficult for a Minister who had allowed his Civil Servants to become dominant to disguise that fact. The exacting barrage of criticism from the Opposition, on major bills at least, leaves little hope of concealing ignorance. The Civil Servants provide the explanatory memoranda for the Minister's use to clarify difficult passages in the bill, but that is the limit of their influence. The crucial question of whether the bill will pass its Second Reading stage is decided not by the clarity of its wording, but by factors involving party loyalty and party policy over which Civil Servants have no influence at all. The Committee stage with its detailed analysis of each clause of the bill gives more opportunity for Civil Service influence. Civil Servants do not intervene directly in proceedings, but are present in the Committee room, and the Minister will often choose to consult them on the practical wisdom of accepting proposed amendments. This advice they are well-qualified to give from their long experience of assessing the probable administrative difficulties involved in making Parliamentary legislation work in practice. It is the Minister who decides, however, whether to accept their advice and it is the M.P.s serving on the Committee who decide by their votes what alterations shall be made at the Committee stage; these alterations are concerned with wording, not with the general import and principles of the bill. The Report and Third Reading stages are brief. M.P.s may introduce additional amendments at the Report stage and this could lead to further consultations between the Minister and Civil Servant advisers, who are present in the House of Commons behind the Speaker's Chair, but in general these last stages of the bill are considerably less important than the Second Reading and Committee stages.

Assuming that the bill is introduced in the House of Commons, it then has to go through the same stages in the House of Lords. Since most Ministers are in the House of Commons it will often be necessary to nominate a Peer to pilot the bill through its various stages in the House of Lords. The growth of the practice of using Ministers of State as official deputies to the fully-fledged Ministers has made it easier to find in both Houses members with detailed knowledge of departmental work. This, in turn, makes it easier to ensure a smooth passage through the second House, since, if the Peer in charge of the bill is imperfectly acquainted with departmental practice, or has little prior acquaintance with the bill, this increases the responsibility of the Civil Servants concerned. Their advice will become correspondingly important, but the general form of the bill will already have been decided in its passage through the Lower House; any amendments introduced in the Lords, and subsequently rejected by the Commons, become the subject of consultation between the two Houses, so that there is no opportunity for unilateral action by Civil Service advisers.

Once the bill has gained Royal Assent, and the Minister has appointed the day when it will come into force, the Statutory Instruments, that is, the detailed regulations necessary to make the Act work, have to be issued, and the responsibility for devising them rests very largely on the Civil Service. It would be inappropriate and time-devouring for Parliament to concern itself with detail of this kind. Even in the nineteenth century, when political life was more leisurely and Statutory Instruments less numerous, matters of administrative detail were not normally considered by Parliament. There are a host of matters nowadays, such as insurance contributions and exceptions, national assistance, and health regulations, where either the complexity of the issue or the need for speedy action makes it expedient to rely on the specialist knowledge of Civil Servants. Their decisions are limited, however, by the fact that they cannot act beyond the scope of the powers conferred by the parent Act.

In addition, there are Parliamentary Committees specifically required to scrutinise Statutory Instruments. The House of Lords has had a Special Orders Committee since 1925. More important is the Scrutiny Committee set up by the House of Commons in 1944. This Committee is required according to its terms of reference, 'to consider every Statutory Instrument laid or laid in draft before the House . . . with a view to determining whether the special attention of the House should be drawn to it on any of the following grounds . . .', and these grounds, comprising broadly any irregular or unusual feature in the Instrument, are then stated. The findings of the Committee may lead to the moving of a prayer in the House of Commons to annul an unsatisfactory order. As a matter of

Parliamentary convention members of the Committee itself are not expected to move these prayers, since their function is conceived simply in terms of the provision of information upon which other members may act. Otherwise criticism of a Minister by members of the Committee might be interpreted as part of a deliberately conceived campaign. Considering that there have been many thousands of Statutory Instruments since 1945, the numbers reported by the Committee for the attention of the House are very few, frequently less than ten a year. But the work of the Committee should not be under-rated. Apart from the possibility of causing action to be taken in the House of Commons over a particular order, the Committee has the power to issue statements on general principles relating to the issue of Statutory Instruments. These principles based on detailed observations of the form of the Instruments are valuable for the guidance of Civil Servants, as well as being, in effect, a means of circumscribing their authority in their subsequent attempts to devise the wording of Instruments satisfactorily. Civil Servants are keenly aware of the need to avoid actions likely to be criticised in Parliamentary Committees, and possibly in Parliament itself subsequently. This state of mind is produced not only by the fear that such criticism may jeopardise their careers, but also by the realisation apt to be felt in any historic organisation that actions are conditioned by tradition. In Britain the weight of tradition is heavily in favour of Civil Service dependence on Parliamentary authority. It is true, however, that Civil Servants have great powers of initiation of these Instruments within the terms of the parent Act. The extent to which Statutory Instruments can be made to work fairly depends, in the first place, on the approach of Civil Servants to their responsibilities, and on well-informed supervision by the Minister of the work of his Department.

There are some risks, therefore, that Civil Service influence on the making of Statutory Instruments may be imperfectly controlled, but in the devising of the parent Act the Government and the Minister must clearly have the dominant role. This does not accurately describe the situation where financial bills are involved since, in this respect, Treasury influence is very great indeed; its views are an important consideration also in deciding the fate of other bills which involve the spending of public money. The question of the relationship of the Treasury to Parliament is of extreme importance, and merits more detailed examination than is possible within the space of this chapter (see Chapter 6). Recent Government policy and the expertise of the Treasury have given the latter body greater dominance than ever in financial affairs.

Apart from its work in connection with legislation the Civil Service has several other general administrative duties to perform. These duties give scope for decisions which may be resented, and it is in this sphere of activity that concern for individual rights has been most strongly felt in recent years. Surrounded by able and well-informed Civil Service advisers the Minister will feel amply justified in delegating to them important responsibilities. Senior Civil Servants will meet representatives of industry and local government for an exchange of views on the implications in practice of departmental policy. The Civil Servants may well have to give some guidance to those they meet, and, at the same time, discussions with the men and women who are experiencing the effects of Government decisions will give the Civil Servants an opportunity at first hand to assess the merits of that policy. The outcome of the meeting will be a report to the Minister and, if he feels it necessary, further meetings at which he himself may preside. There is a chance that a Minister, lacking in zeal or in time, may increasingly delegate this liaison work to Civil Servants so that his supervision becomes purely nominal. They will then, in effect, be discharging his powers, and, confident in the knowledge gained from their meetings with the various outside organisations, will have a rapidly diminishing respect for the ability of their Minister to give sound decisions. This is the situation which can come about through inadequate Ministerial supervision. It is not that the Civil Servants are consciously seeking power, but simply that the vacuum created by inadequate leadership will be filled by the expansion of the powers of the Civil Service, so that the processes of government may continue effectively. Nor is it at all certain that the Civil Servants would perform their additional responsibilities with any less wisdom and fairness than the Minister. It is certain, however, that the Civil Servants, sheltered by their anonymity and comparative immunity from the risk of dismissal, are much less vulnerable, and therefore much less sensitive, to public opinion than their politician Minister. Since our constitutional system is based on the ultimate accountability of the Government to the people it is undesirable that Civil Servants should have much freedom of decision in administration. While it is unfair to describe them as 'paper workers', seeing little company except their own kind, it is true that those whom they meet are the more able, influential, and persuasive members of the community: sensitivity to the feelings of the masses, essential for the politician, is not a necessity for the Civil Servant. This is why it can be dangerous for a Minister to delegate too extensively to his Civil Servants powers of policy decision and interpretation. There are checks which can be imposed, as will be seen later, but these will generally operate after, and because some damage has already been done.

The danger of Civil Service influence becoming unduly assertive in the co-ordination meetings with group organisations is only one of the factors producing concern. These meetings, after all, are only to implement and interpret policies which have already been approved: even so they should be closely supervised by the Minister. A more dangerous situation is produced when the Civil Servants are in a position when they virtually initiate decisions. Private Bill procedure, which can be expensive and slow, has been partly superseded in recent years by the growing use of Provisional Orders, which are subject to Parliamentary approval later. A local authority may apply for a Provisional Order, or a Government Department itself may by means of a draft order secure powers to make possible some project, such as a large-scale road-building scheme envisaged by the Ministry of Transport. The effective power of decision rests with the Minister, but Civil Service influence can play a greater or lesser part in the decision according to the relationship of the Minister and his advisers. Parliament must give its attention predominantly to national matters, and the intensity of scrutiny it can bring to bear on these decisions in local matters is not very great, until after some complaint has already arisen. There are means of making public objection to orders of this kind, but these means are often only imperfectly understood, and the individual citizen is apt to be out of his element in disputes with the experts. A road-building scheme, in particular, will almost certainly involve acquisition of land by means of Compulsory Purchase Orders and these, too, have frequently been a subject of complaint, partly because of their infringement of individual freedom, partly because the compensation given to the owner has fallen short of the price to be obtained from a normal private sale on the open market.

The powers of compulsion vested in Government Departments

have grown in recent years with the increasing centralisation of administration, and the tacit acceptance of the fact that administrative efficiency may make necessary further reductions of individual liberties. It has led to the ejection of farmers on the grounds that they are incapable of performing their work effectively, and it has led twice in recent years to serious Parliamentary concern over departmental powers for the compulsory acquisition of land. The first occasion concerned some seven hundred acres of land at Crichel Down which had originally been acquired by the Air Ministry in 1937 by compulsory purchase. After the war the land was handed over to the Ministry of Agriculture. It was decided by this Ministry to let the land, which was a perfectly reasonable decision, although many people, including a Lieutenant-Commander Marten, were hoping for an outright sale. Marten's father-in-law had owned some of the original acreage acquired by the Air Ministry in 1937. A tenant was then found, recommended by the estate agents acting on behalf of the Permanent Commissioners of Crown Lands. The Civil Servants at the Ministry of Agriculture failed to inform the prospective purchasers, as they should have done, of their proposed action, and these people felt that the omission to do so was irregular and high-handed. Marten, in particular, was given active support by several M.P.s in pressing the matter in the House of Commons, where, following unsatisfactory answers at Question-time, a full debate took place. Pressure in the House of Commons by supporters of Lieutenant-Commander Marten led to the appointment of a judicial inquiry. When the report was published, criticism of the Minister and of senior Civil Servants was so pointed that Sir Thomas Dugdale, then Minister of Agriculture, felt obliged to resign. The case roused considerable concern and led to the issue of a warning to Civil Servants by the Permanent Secretary to the Treasury of the dangers involved in any abuse of their powers. Furthermore, one of the Civil Servants involved was transferred to other duties. The situation was the more disquieting in that the actions of the Ministry might not have been effectively challenged at all had it not been for the energetic persistence of Lieutenant-Commander Marten.

More recently the sale by the Air Ministry to an aircraft company of a large area of agricultural land at Chalgrove, requisitioned from the owners, caused sufficient concern to make it the subject of an Adjournment Debate, and some measure of adverse Press publicity. The original owners believed that they should have been given the option of re-purchase, and were not reassured by the statement that the aircraft company would not require the land for longer than a period of five years. The use of these acres by an aircraft company has also involved the closing of the old highway, questions of rights of way across the aerodrome, and controversy about the siting of possible alternative routes. There have been a number of other instances in recent years, admirably surveyed by T. E. Utley's book *Occasion for Ombudsman*,[1] when decisions by the Executive have borne very heavily upon the individual citizen. The extent to which Parliament can effectively intervene will be examined in the next chapter, but the inescapable fact that hardship to individuals has occurred makes it plain that no panacea has yet been found for misguided actions by the Executive. The Minister of the Department concerned is ultimately responsible, but it is doubtful whether he can always be fully aware of all the implications of decisions which he must, to some extent, delegate to his senior Civil Servants; the Crichel Down case added to these doubts. It is quite evident that changing circumstances have conspired to give senior Civil Servants a fuller share in policy decisions than was customary before the war.

In order to deal with objections by citizens against policies which may be injurious to them, several Departments make use of administrative tribunals. They have been used since the war for matters such as appeals for deferment of national service, for hearing objections to development plans, and for problems involving pensions and national insurance. These tribunals are recognised to be necessary. The probable alternative would be to make use of the law-courts, but this would lead to an undesirable congestion of business there, and would be fundamentally inappropriate since decisions at these tribunals are not judicial in the fullest sense; they have to be based at times on expediency, and for their settlement require the detailed expert knowledge of the departmental officials. Moreover, the flexibility and informality of administrative tribunal procedure may well be advantageous to the citizen whose interests are affected. The boundaries of a judge's authority are limited by statutes and Common Law, but tribunal

---

[1] Ombudsman: an official used in Denmark, Sweden, and New Zealand to scrutinise complaints against the effects of administrative decisions by Government Departments (see p. 73).

members have greater scope for avoiding a mechanical interpretation of the laws. This greater discretion, however, carries with it greater risks, and emphasises the need for close Ministerial and Parliamentary supervision. The safeguards which are so scrupulously provided in a court of law were very imperfectly applied until the Government implemented the main recommendations embodied in the report made by the Franks Committee in 1957. Previously the citizen, lacking legal representation and adequate knowledge of the issues involved, was often unable to state his case properly, and an imperfect appeal system, which gave the Minister appellate powers in matters concerning his own Department, meant that the danger of unfair decisions was greatly magnified.

Those recommendations of the Franks Report acceptable to the Government were embodied in the Tribunals and Inquiries Act of 1958, and the Town and Country Planning Act of 1959. By the former act a Council on Tribunals for England, Wales, and Scotland was set up, appointed jointly by the Lord Chancellor and by the Secretary of State for Scotland; its purpose is to exercise general oversight over the composition and procedure of tribunals. The Franks Committee had advocated that tribunal proceedings should be based on the three principles of openness, fairness, and impartiality. The detailed application of these principles in practice could obviously not be defined by statute alone, but Ministries have brought these principles specifically to the notice of officials involved in tribunal work. The Act also effected an improvement in that members of the public concerned now receive much fuller information than before about the reasons for Compulsory Purchase Orders, and the reasons for refusal of planning permission. In connection with the latter there is, under the Town and Country Planning Act of 1959, a right of appeal to the courts when planning permission is refused.

This recent legislation has strengthened the position of the citizen in relation to Government Department decisions, but defects still remain. One of these springs from the fact that the Franks Committee was limited in its terms of reference to considering defects evident in quasi-judicial procedure. Many administrative decisions involve no such formal mechanism and as Mr. Utley has pointed out, 'it cannot be made too clear that the Committee did not consider such circumstances as those of Crichel

Down within its terms of reference'.[1] Another possible weakness in the present situation concerns appeal procedure. Appeals to courts of law, or to superior tribunals, are not absolutely debarred. There are difficulties to be considered, however. Appeals to the courts may only be on a point of law, and tribunal decisions may well produce a strong sense of grievance without infringement of the law. Appeals to superior tribunals are only possible when there exists a definite hierarchy of tribunals. It may happen, for example, that a tribunal of first instance is very strongly composed in its membership, and in that event there may not be a superior tribunal. It should be added, in fairness, that unlimited freedom of appeal would be very time-wasting, and that the courts of law are by their nature far better fitted to deal with the legal matters which are rarely in dispute than they are with the discretionary judgments which are much more frequently controversial. A further protection for the citizen exists in the fact that appeals are now more likely to go to an appellate tribunal rather than to the Minister himself, though this is not invariable. Furthermore the Council on Tribunals is empowered to propose new rules for the conduct of tribunal proceedings, thus giving further scope for improving the situation.

Striking a balance between the rights of the citizen and administrative convenience is far from easy however. The report of the Council on Tribunals (March, 1962) on the Essex 'chalk-pit case' has given some insight into the problems which can still arise. A company, known as Heath and Son, Ltd., was refused permission by the Saffron Waldon Council to work chalk on land in Essex on the grounds that the chalk-dust would be detrimental to pigs and ponies on the adjacent land. An inspector's inquiry supported the Council's view. The company appealed against this decision and, after a ten months' delay, the Minister of Housing and Local Government allowed the appeal, following consultation with the Minister of Agriculture. One of the objectors to the chalk-pit working, a Major Buxton, appealed to the High Court against the Ministry decision, but the High Court could find no legal basis for action. To the objectors the disturbing feature about the case was the way in which further advice was taken by the Minister of Housing and Local Government, namely from the Minister of Agriculture. It was felt that this fresh advice should either have

[1] T. E. Utley, *Occasion for Ombudsman*, p. 27.

been obtained earlier so that it might have been made known at the inspector's inquiry, or that a fresh inquiry should have been started so that the parties concerned might state their views on this advice from the Ministry of Agriculture. The essence of the matter was the old maxim that justice should not only be done but that it should be seen to be done. This was apparently the view of the Council on Tribunals. Following the case it proposed that when the Minister intends to disagree with his inspector's recommendation he will notify the parties concerned so that they can protest before a decision is made. Furthermore if fresh evidence becomes available after an inquiry any of the parties can ask for a re-opening of the inquiry.

It is evident from the practices considered in this chapter that the Executive has considerable latitude in making decisions. It is the more important, therefore, that the relationship of the Minister to his Civil Servants should be closely defined so that responsibility for actions can be fairly assigned. This does not remove the possibility of maladministration but makes it less likely. This was more fully realised after the Crichel Down case, and Sir David Maxwell Fyfe, then Home Secretary, made a statement defining Ministerial Responsibility in this connection.[1] From this it became clear that if a Civil Servant is merely carrying out an order given by the Minister the latter must obviously bear full responsibility. This responsibility is hardly, if at all, diminished if the Civil Servant's action is in accordance with the known policy of the Minister. The Civil Servant has to use some degree of initiative in decisions, and if he acts in good faith, as he believes the Minister would wish him to do, it would be unsatisfactory for the Minister to shield himself by disowning responsibility for the action. On the other hand, there are occasions in large and busy Government Departments when Civil Servants exceed their authority and act in a way of which the Minister would certainly disapprove. It may be a relatively minor fault which is exposed, as, for instance, when the stationery of one Government Department was used by an employee on a recent occasion for distributing party propaganda. The Minister cannot be held responsible for every peccadillo committed by the thousands employed in his Ministry. He must, however, explain the position to Parliament and take the necessary corrective action. The same principle applies if a major fault in the working of a Govern-

---

[1] House of Commons Debate, July 20th, 1954, cols. 1285 ff.

ment Department is exposed. If it is sufficiently serious the Minister may feel obliged to resign, as Sir Thomas Dugdale did after the Crichel Down episode. On the other hand, the defection of Burgess and Maclean to Russia, though obviously of serious importance, could not reasonably be made the occasion for censure of the Minister or Civil Servants, since the Fuchs case and other comparable examples since the war have shown how easy it is for individuals to conceal their political allegiance from those with whom they work.

The doctrine of Ministerial Responsibility, therefore, has to be applied with some discrimination, but there is no doubt that it is taken seriously. This is a factor of considerable importance in assessing the relationship of the Minister to his Civil Servants and is buttressed by the fact that the Minister, in conjunction with the Treasury, has effective powers of discipline over his Department. It is important to realise also that Ministerial Responsibility does not only apply when some aspect of maladministration is publicly revealed. It is a factor which must influence the whole day-to-day management of the Department. Lord Morrison in *Government and Parliament* makes it plain that Civil Servants prefer to have a vigilant and energetic Minister,[1] and a Minister with these qualities, from his wide experience of the practical effects of policy decisions, will often be able to give valuable guidance to Civil Servants, thus removing by anticipation any undesirable features from administrative decisions. This is the best form of Ministerial Responsibility.

In this chapter the main purpose has been to examine the relationship of the Minister to his Civil Servants. The influence of the latter over non-financial bills is normally slight; in this respect, they have a useful but subordinate role. They have wide powers in the devising of Statutory Instruments, and it is difficult for Parliament to supervise all the details involved in this form of delegated legislation. Over financial matters their power is very great, as will be seen later. Also in matters of policy decision the situation has dangers since basically it rests in the variable factor of the relationship between the Civil Servant and his Minister. It is some protection that the Civil Service itself has a tradition of impartial administration, and that the Permanent Secretary to the Treasury has disciplinary powers over Civil Servants, as the Ministers have

[1] *Ibid.*, Ch. XIV.

also. These internal factors may modify policy decisions in favour of the citizen, but are insufficient in themselves as absolute guarantees of individual rights. Whether such guarantees exist for the citizen in his relationship both with the Departments and with the Government remains to be seen in the next chapter.

FURTHER READING

Lord Morrison, *Government and Parliament* (O.U.P., 3rd Edition, 1964).
T. A. Critchley, *The Civil Service Today* (Gollancz, 1951).
G. A. Campbell, *The Civil Service in Britain* (Pelican Books, 1955).
T. E. Utley, *Occasion for Ombudsman* (Johnson, 1961).
    See also Comments on Further Reading, p. 165.

The Redress of Grievances

Historical basis for the redress of grievances. Methods of expressing grievances and an assessment of their worth: letters, lobbying, Parliamentary Questions, petitions, pressure-groups. The possibility of legislative action. The historic freedoms and their present-day relevance. Additional protection needed for the citizen in modern conditions. An Ombudsman and the alternatives.

THEME: The traditional guarantees of citizens' freedoms are losing their effectiveness and new forms of protection are required.

The increasing power of the Executive in modern times is only too apparent; yet in Britain law, strongly reinforced by custom, secures essential freedoms for the citizen. Moreover, the long struggle for supremacy between the monarchy and Parliament in the seventeenth century was based in the first place on the principle that there should be 'redress of grievances before supply'. In defending its own constitutional rights so zealously Parliament was also fighting the war on behalf of the individual citizen. It is obvious that Parliament was not a fully representative institution in the seventeenth century, and was not to be so until universal franchise was achieved in 1928, yet some of the principles secured during the struggle with the Stuart Kings, such as freedom of speech in Parliament, the abolition of prerogative courts, and the removal of royal authority to levy taxes, concerned the citizen as much as they concerned the position of Parliament in the constitution. In demanding that redress of grievances should precede supply the Parliamentarians were thinking of their own position in relation to the monarchy; the benefit to the mass of the citizens was incidental but no less real. In modern times there has been a change of outlook. Parliament still has the duty of acting as a check on any abuse of authority by the Executive, that is, the

Government and its various subordinate instruments of power, but in this capacity nowadays M.P.s are less conscious of constitutional rivalry with the Executive and more aware of the need to give the fullest ventilation to the grievances of citizens. The extension of the vote has obviously had some influence in this respect. It would appear, therefore, that there are strong historical, legal, and practical grounds for expecting that a citizen with a grievance against the Government would command vigorous support in the House of Commons.

Assuming then that a citizen has a grievance against any manifestation of Government activity he will probably seek a remedy first by writing to the Government Department concerned. Sometimes, if there are local offices of the relevant Ministry, the citizen may call there to discuss his grievance. Should these procedures fail to give him satisfaction he may then have recourse to a number of other methods. If his grievance is shared by many others, as it might be, for instance, if pits were closed down by the National Coal Board, then deputations of miners to the Coal Board, and to lobby M.P.s at Westminster are possible. Lobbying has become a familiar routine in recent years; it has been used by miners, teachers, and car-workers amongst others. There is no decisive evidence to indicate that it is a successful method of remedying complaints. It gives them a brief publicity, soon submerged in the flood of world news which pours out every day from radio, television and the Press. In a sense it can be argued that lobbying is almost an admission of defeat, a desperate expedient devised to stimulate M.P.s into more vigorous action than they would be likely to undertake in the ordinary way. Very often lobbying simply underlines the obvious, that a certain group of the community is discontented with some aspect of Government policy. M.P.s will know this already, and, as lobbying is generally employed over matters where a firm Government decision has recently been made, neither Government supporters nor the Opposition can do very much about it. Lobbying, therefore, seems an empty form of protest so far as securing a remedy is concerned, though it may make some M.P.s more vividly aware of the nature of the grievance than they were before.

It is also possible for groups or for individuals to write to or visit their M.P. privately in the hope that he will act as an intermediary for their complaint. He may either write to the Minister concerned, or, if this fails to produce satisfaction, he may ask a question in the House of Commons. It was in this latter way, for instance, that the Crichel Down case, mentioned in the last chapter, was first forced upon the attention of the House of Commons. Grievances are not always so spectacular, but they may be equally important for the individuals concerned. A refusal by a Service unit to grant compassionate leave, for instance, will only affect a very small number of people, but it could well be the subject of a Parliamentary question. There are occasions when a question in the House is an effective way of dealing with a complaint. This is particularly so when it can be demonstrated that the complaint stems from highhanded actions by the Executive. To demonstrate this is far from easy, however, for the administrators are likely to have a more detailed knowledge of their powers than the individual has of his rights. Moreover, as a Parliamentary question is sometimes a last resort following a long period of correspondence, concessions by the Minister answering the questions are by no means certain. By means of supplementary questions, allowed at the discretion of the Speaker, the questioner may be able to put the Minister at such a disadvantage that he can successfully press for the matter to be raised again in the Debate on the Adjournment. Factors other than the merits of the issue, however, such as the availability of Parliamentary time and the power of a well-prepared Ministerial answer to avoid controversy, have a bearing on whether the matter is likely to be discussed again. At one extreme, therefore, the Parliamentary question can be a very damp squib in which an M.P. raises the issue, the Minister gives a smooth but not very revealing answer, the M.P. follows with an ironic or critical supplementary question, and there the matter rests. At the other extreme a question may touch on a matter so fundamental that the Government may appoint a Committee of Inquiry and its report may well lead to new legislation. The setting-up of the Franks Committee on Administrative Tribunals and the resulting legislation provide an example of this process. In general, however, it would be unduly complacent to believe that Question-time in the House provides a universal remedy for all grievances.

It is possible that a Parliamentary question which does not receive a satisfactory answer may become the subject of the Debate on the Adjournment. As the Whyatt Report[1] points out, the pro-

---

[1] *The Citizen and the Administration* — a report by Justice, pp. 38–44.

cedural apparatus both for the Parliamentary question and the Debate on the Adjournment is imperfectly adjusted for the redress of grievances springing from a dispute between a Government Department and a citizen. The essential weakness is embodied in the Report's comment that 'the proceedings which began as an investigation have turned into a contest in which the spokesman on each side identifies himself with his cause and consequently it is rare for either side to give any ground; moreover it is often an uneven contest in the sense that the Minister has access to documents and information which are denied to his opponent'.[1] The most conspicuous criticism of a Parliamentary tug-of-war of this kind is that the procedure is simply not appropriate to the problem raised. There is admittedly the further expedient of an *ad hoc* inquiry ordered by the Government on matters considered sufficiently important. Yet this is too monumental a process to be used very often and is clearly of remote value to the citizen suffering from hardship of individual but not national importance.

The other means of securing Parliamentary redress of grievances are more circuitous, and some of them probably of negligible value. Petitions have a respectable ancestry. In the early history of Parliament, in the fourteenth century, petitions were the normal method of drawing attention to grievances. Later on they reached their most spectacular form in the bulky petitions presented by the Chartists to the House of Commons in 1839 and 1842. The frivolous forgery of signatures and the theatrical method of presentation brought petitions into disrepute. In modern times the details of the form and presentation of petitions have been rigidly prescribed. They are occasionally used still. Some citizens of Orpington, for instance, sent a petition to Parliament in February, 1962, praying for an early by-election, on the grounds that they had had no M.P. since the resignation of their previous representative some months before. Petitions are not a very convincing form of argument however. The motives for signing them may be very mixed and they are accordingly liable to be received with some cynicism by the House. In an educated and politically informed society the mere accumulation of signatures does not significantly add to the force of the arguments used, and the petition procedure seems almost archaic.

Special interest groups — the 'pressure-groups' — are more

[1] *Ibid.*, p. 41.

effective in the removal of specific grievances, though, as has been seen (Chapter 2), their influence on policy-making is much less certain. They vary enormously in size. There are the Trade Unions which sponsor approximately 100 Labour M.P.s, the Co-operative Societies, which are also an integral part of Labour Party organisation, professional associations such as the National Union of Teachers and the National Association of Local Government Officers, which are not committed to any one political party, groups such as the Federation of British Industries, whose interests lie with the Conservative Party, and a large number of small societies such as the Lord's Day Observance Society and the Anti-Vivisection League which are concerned with narrower objectives. The term 'pressure-group' is sometimes used with a rather sinister connotation, as if M.P.s were no more than ventriloquists' dummies, the uncritical mouthpieces of shadowy groups whose activities are none too clearly discerned. 'Pressure-group' is, however, simply a new name for a very old form of activity. The Church, the barons, and landowners have all belonged to pressure-groups in the past and provided a greater threat to social progress than the pressure-groups of the present day. Sometimes these groups have been the source of valuable reforms. The emancipation of women, for instance, came about through the persistent advocacy and action of groups such as the National Society for Women's Suffrage founded in 1867, and the Women's Social and Political Union founded in 1903. The tactics of the extreme suffragettes may have been faulty, but the existence of these organisations undoubtedly hastened the movement towards greater equality of the sexes.

The great advantage which these groups have over the individual is that Governments are much more likely to take account of their influence in modifying legislation. The possibility of an individual being able to influence Government legislation can be almost discounted. If his grievance is such that it needs new legislation to remove it, his prospects of success are slight. He may be able to induce some appropriate authority to introduce a Private Bill, but because of the expense involved in employing counsel and summoning witnesses at the Committee stage if the bill is opposed, this is not a very popular form of action. It is conceivable, but highly improbable, that an M.P. would see in the grievance of a constituent a general defect in the national system which could be righted by a Private Member's Bill; but he would have to be lucky in the ballot for the right to introduce such a bill, and he would have to be luckier still to manage the difficult process of getting the bill through all its stages in Parliament. So far as a citizen has any personal initiative in righting a grievance it is plain that his best chance, by far, will be to join a group or society to press his claims. Otherwise, in the procedures available to the individual citizen there are elements of chance which make it uncertain whether satisfaction can always be given.

It is true, however, that the initiative in the removal of grievances does not always have to come from the citizen himself. It has been indicated already in the chapter on the Civil Service (Chapter 4) that by means of the doctrine of Ministerial Responsibility, and by means of the Statutory Instruments Committee, the Government and Parliament can protect the citizen against abuses by Executive officials. In addition, it is often asserted in admiration of the British constitution that, while there has been little attempt to define with legal precision the liberties of the subject, these liberties are more effectively secured by the atmosphere of public opinion than they could possibly be by Parliamentary statute. There are a few historic documents, such as the Habeas Corpus Act (1679), which have attempted to give documentary form to some of the essential liberties. Common law decisions also provide a point of reference in determining the liberties of the subject. It would be impossible, however, to give a satisfactory account of all the individual liberties by reference to statutes or common law decisions alone. Both statutes and law courts are subject to the authority of Parliament, and, to give one instance, the principle of fair judicial proceedings, which was one of the aims of the makers of Magna Charta (though only for their own class), was blatantly disregarded time and again in subsequent years. The links between past Acts of Parliament and the contemporary approach to individual liberties are apt to be somewhat tenuous. This has led to a flexibility in the interpretation of the rights of the individual citizen which is generally held to be greatly to his advantage. In theory, the absolute sovereignty of Parliament, now largely superseded by Cabinet dominance, could be indistinguishable from despotism between one election and another, and elections themselves could be made subject to governmental wishes; in practice, respect for individual rights is so ingrained that abuses of governmental power would appear as reprehensible to those who govern as to those who are governed.

If this were an entirely accurate assessment of the relationship between Government and the citizen there would be little cause for concern. Even if the various procedures for protection of the individual were imperfect in themselves, and there is some reason for believing that this is so, no serious harm could result since the long-established freedoms of the subject would be inviolable. To some extent this is true. Freedoms which no longer involve any challenge to Executive authority, such as freedom of religion, are firmly entrenched. It would be foolish to pretend, however, that in modern times all the traditional freedoms are secure from challenge. There are mounting pressures in world affairs, and in changing economic conditions, which make it expedient to strengthen the hand of the Executive, and this may increasingly involve infringements on the freedom of action of individuals. In Victorian times the extent of planning and control now accepted as natural by all the main parties would have been regarded as being out of character completely with the nature of the British constitution and, to that extent, abhorrent. However, opinion on the essential nature of the British constitution changes markedly, not only from century to century, but within much shorter intervals also. Since the last war there have been developments which clearly impinge on the liberties of the subject. These developments are not spectacular, but they are important.

The most conspicuous example of change is that the right to free possession of personal property is no longer regarded as sacrosanct. In former times, the English roads meandered on their course in deference to the sacred property rights of the English landowners, who preferred to keep the roads outside the boundaries of their estate. Railway stations in the nineteenth century were often sited inconveniently on the outskirts of cities in order to placate local hostility to these new mechanical horrors. Nowadays, Governments launching out on great road-schemes, or on the extension of the national grid system for the provision of electricity, are unlikely to be deterred by the obstinacy of a few freeholders. Compulsory Purchase Orders give the necessary sanction required. There is, admittedly, the possibility of a public inquiry attended by the Ministry Inspectors. The paramount need for an efficient road system, and for improved amenities, such as the supply of electricity, makes it unlikely that the objecting citizen will be able to press his claim with much hope of success. Diversions of proposed routes involve heavy additional expense, to be faced ultimately by the taxpayer, and it is highly probable that objections will be swallowed up by considerations of the general benefits of the proposed scheme for large sections of the community. All this is natural and understandable, but also much more frequent in recent years. It is fair to add that the Government has shown itself alive to the hardships which may be created by planned development. The Electricity Act of 1957, for instance, incorporated greater safeguards for those whose land was likely to be affected by extensions of the national grid system. This was brought about largely by the prolonged struggle between a Surrey farmer, Mr. Dudley Glanfield, and the Central Electricity Authority over the erection of a pylon line across his land.[1] It is disquieting that in this incident, as in others, legislation has followed a complaint, not removed it by anticipation. The power of the Ministry of Agriculture to evict inefficient farmers is another instance of the way in which the power of the Executive has intruded upon the full and free use of personal property; moreover, it is not a dormant power for it has been invoked, though rarely.

While it is generally conceded that governmental powers have extended in this way, it is often argued that the citizen in a modern community expects Government management of the economy and of social services, and is prepared in the interests of the community to accept the slight risk of some loss of personal rights. Besides he has other relevant privileges such as the right, since the 1947 Crown Proceedings Act, to sue a Government Department; the existence of an impartial judicial system is a further reassurance that soundly-based complaints will receive the consideration they deserve. Beyond these protections he has the privilege of free speech so that the attention of Parliament may be brought to the grievance of any citizen. In fact there are limitations to these privileges. The Courts are themselves subordinate to Parliament in the sense that they can only ensure that a Government Department has conducted its procedures in accordance with the terms laid down in the relevant statute. This may or may not be preferable to a system in which a wholly independent Judiciary could hamper the full application of Parliamentary statute by reference to principles of justice of its own

[1] T. E. Utley, *Occasion for Ombudsman*, pp. 68–77.

devising. Whatever the opinion may be on this, it does not alter the
fact that in the present system the principle of the equality of all
men before the law, which is ideally desirable, cannot be applicable
when the dispute is between a citizen and a Government Department. The latter is inevitably placed in a position of superiority
through having been associated itself, through its Minister, with
the process of law-making. Furthermore Government Departments may withhold evidence if they wish in the interests of State
security, of which they must necessarily be the judges themselves.
The Government, too, has powers to strengthen its position against
individual claims by further legislation. There may be sound reasons
for all these advantages, but a dispute between a Government Department and a citizen can hardly be conducted on the same level of
equality as a dispute between citizens. It is true, however, that there
is a further protection for the citizen, the privilege of free speech.

Freedom of speech is so basic a part of the British tradition that
it has acquired a sentimental aura making perception of reality
more difficult. Most people are familiar with the endearing story of
the policeman silencing a heckler so that he may give undivided
attention to the soap-box orator in Hyde Park furiously attacking
the forces of law and order which the policeman himself represents.
There is a sense of insular superiority about the policeman's
amiable tolerance. From the incident one is expected to deduce the
willingness of Government and of its officials to accept criticism
without victimising the critics. It is possible to make a deduction of
quite another kind from these facts, however, namely that the
course and actions of the Government are unlikely to be altered one
iota by self-appointed orators, and freedom of speech of this traditional kind is of negligible importance. It acts, as has been often
said, as a safety-valve for society, but the real point of the comparison is that the steam which escapes through a safety-valve is simply
wasted. Free speech, in the other sense, involving approach directly
to Government Departments, or indirectly through Parliament by
means of M.P.s acting on behalf of their constituents to remedy
grievances, does not mean that a satisfactory solution can always be
found. Parliament is overworked. Probably it is largely for this
reason that the devices for bringing a private or group grievance to
public notice, such as lobbying, getting questions asked in Parliament, and so on, cannot be guaranteed to be effective, as was seen
earlier in this chapter.

F

There have been a number of incidents in recent years, many of which are very fully described in T. E. Utley's *Occasion for Ombudsman*, where Government Department decisions have involved hardship for citizens which might have been avoided. Human failings are inevitable in any great organisation where thousands are employed. The citizen is far more likely to acquire a sense of grievance against Civil Service decisions in the lower levels of Departments than he is on matters of sufficient importance to move Parliament strongly to action. Undoubtedly, too, he will often be deterred by the difficulties involved in remedying his grievance through the ordinary processes of Parliament. Lord Shawcross in his preface to the Whyatt Report uses the cogent phrase that 'the little farmer with four acres and a cow would never have attempted to force the battlements of Crichel Down'.[1] Obviously there have been many occasions when the existing procedure of letters to Departments, questions in the House, and so on have led to satisfactory remedies for the citizen; but increasing pressure on Parliamentary time, inadequacies of procedure, and the extension of Government administrative activity, often of great complexity, have combined to make Parliament a less effective watchdog of citizens' rights than it used to be.

Various remedies have been proposed. In France, the Conseil d'État,[2] which dates back to Napoleon's time, can act on behalf of a citizen with a grievance against an administrative decision. It is itself composed of Civil Servants, but its traditional concern for fair administration makes this no bar to the conscientious discharge of its duties. It has power to override Government Department decisions, which makes its position akin to that of a Supreme Court. Its powers over administrative decisions are wider, in fact, than those of the Supreme Court in the United States, since it makes its decisions not on the authority of constitutional statements but on the more flexible authority of natural justice. Mr. Utley convincingly points out that we could scarcely create the equivalent of a Conseil d'État in Britain since this would give too much untrammelled power to an unrepresentative group of officials.[3]

---

[1] *Ibid.*, p. xiii.

[2] *Conseil d'État* — supreme court of appeal for administrative matters.

[3] For this point, and for an assessment of the value of an Ombudsman in Britain, together with the possible alternatives, see T. E. Utley, *Occasion for Ombudsman*, particularly pp. 135–44.

The Danes and Swedes use an Ombudsman[1] who, with the necessary office staff, investigates complaints against the Executive, and, though he has no right of direct intervention, can make his decisions and the reasons for them public. This unwanted publicity for bad decisions is a useful means of keeping Government Departments in check. The Ombudsman is appointed by Parliament after each General Election but his independence is secured by statute. His impartiality gives his views more authority than the Press would have by itself. The idea of creating a British equivalent to this official has roused considerable and authoritative support. The Whyatt Report, whose object was to advance suggestions for dealing with those acts of the administration which fell outside the terms of reference of the Franks Committee, proposed that a Parliamentary Commissioner should be appointed. He would investigate complaints of maladministration. He would receive complaints only from members of both Houses of Parliament, though later it might be possible to adapt the system so that members of the public could make their complaints directly to the Commissioner. He would be given reasonable access to departmental files. He would submit both annual and special reports to Parliament. Where the issue was not a matter of maladministration but one where the appropriateness of a discretionary decision was in question, the Whyatt Report suggests that the solution should be the creation of new tribunals, or where this is not practicable the use of a General Tribunal to deal with appeals from miscellaneous discretionary decisions. Matters such as disputes between parents and the local education authority over the choice of schools for children,[2] and *ex gratia* payments by the War Office for damage caused to private property by blast or concussion of guns firing on War Department land,[3] are two of many instances quoted in the Whyatt Report where there is no independent tribunal to arbitrate over discretionary decisions. The extension of the existing tribunal system to provide for discretionary decisions of this type would seem to present little difficulty in principle or in practice. The suggestion for the creation of the office of Parliamentary Commissioner on the other hand involves greater difficulties. There is a reluctance on the part of the Government to give so much influence to one man and, of course, implicitly, to accept that the present Parliamen-

[1] See footnote p. 57.   [2] *Op. cit.*, paragraph 27.
[3] *Op. cit.*, paragraph 42.

tary methods for the redress of grievances are inadequate. The Attorney-General in November, 1962, replying to a question in the House of Commons, defended the existing system and also pointed out that the creation of such an office would conflict with the concept of Ministerial Responsibility.[1]

It may be that Mr. Utley's tentative suggestion that the examination of individual grievances against the Executive should be performed by a House of Commons Committee has more to commend it. This would lead to more systematic examination of grievances than is possible when an M.P. has to act alone in defence of a constituent's interests, and the committee could press for action more effectively than could an M.P. acting on his own. There would be the added advantage, in a country opposed to radical constitutional change, that the creation of a new House of Commons Committee involves little novelty. Increased Executive authority has made it more likely that individual grievances will require greater attention if the democratic system is to work effectively. Abuses of Executive authority have been infrequent so far, but if panic is not justified neither is complacency.

[1] H. C. Debates, November 8th, 1962, cols. 1124–6.

FURTHER READING

D. N. Chester and N. Bowring, *Questions in Parliament* (Oxford — Clarendon Press, 1962).
T. E. Utley, *Occasion for Ombudsman* (Johnson, 1961).
Sir John Whyatt, *The Citizen and the Administration* (Stevens, 1961).
See also Comments on Further Reading, p. 165.

6

The House of Commons
Some Procedural Problems

Shortage of time and the specialisation of knowledge are obstacles to full Parliamentary control. An analysis of legislative procedure suggests that there is little chance of time-saving. This is reinforced by a study of the Select Committee on Procedure proposals of 1958. The inability to adapt procedure to modern conditions has reduced the influence of the House of Commons. Financial procedure is the most conspicuous example of this weakness. Value of a specialist Finance Committee.

THEME: The existing machinery for Parliamentary control is imperfect. Bolder use of Parliamentary committees is a possible solution.

The increasing responsibilities of the Executive would seem to lead to the conclusion that its greater power has been achieved by a reduction in the power of the Legislature. The situation, therefore, could be represented as a simple sum in subtraction. This would be a false simplification, for Parliament works harder than it did before the war, and there has been no formal decree depriving it of its ancient rights. It is possible, alternatively, that the extension in the powers of the Executive has been matched by an extension in the powers of the Legislature; in other words, both branches of government have greater responsibilities. The basis for this belief is that, though governmental control has widened, Parliamentary control, already supposedly strong through the use of questions and open debate, has been tightened still further by new committees, such as those on Statutory Instruments and on Nationalised Industries. It has already been indicated that some procedures, such as Question-time and those involving control of the issue of Statutory Instruments and of Special Orders, can leave loopholes which should be closed. It is fair to point out that the same concern is felt by some M.P.s themselves and has led to the frequent appointment of Select Committees on Procedure to consider suggestions for the more efficient examination of Parliamentary business. Clearly this has the greatest relevance to the extent to which governmental actions can be brought under the scrutiny of Parliament. There are two essential problems. One is how to make more time available to consider the increased volume of legislation of modern times. The second is how to secure stronger Parliamentary control over matters which modern specialisation has made intelligible only to the expert. An outstanding example of the latter problem is national finance. It will be convenient then to consider these two problems in order.

Saving of Parliamentary time is much more difficult to effect than it may appear at first sight. The frequent attempts made by the Select Committees on Procedure, consisting of experienced Parliamentarians, to find a solution suggests that there is little likelihood now of anything except slight changes. Parliamentary procedure, after all, is based on long experience, and for the most part has a sound practical basis. It would be difficult now to bring about changes without intruding on the accepted rights of Parliament. This can be illustrated by an examination of the legislative procedure for a public bill. This process, involving First and Second Readings, Committee, Report, and Third Reading may appear to involve some duplication of effort. There is little substance in this criticism. The First Reading is a brief formality, normally serving no other purpose than to give notice of the important Second Reading stage. This latter stage, the debate on the principles of the bill, is likely to rouse the greatest interest, both among M.P.s and the public. It has been suggested, however, that for less important bills the Second Reading could be taken in Committee. This would virtually mean its removal from the consideration of the House of Commons as a whole, which is undesirable in a democratic system; nor would it be at all easy to define which are the less important bills to the satisfaction of all parties. The content of the bill may give no indication of the issues of principle which may be raised by alert M.P.s, affecting possibly the whole community. While it is possible that Committee members would be equally aware of matters of principle arising out of apparent trivia in legislation, the doctrine of safety in numbers has much to commend it in this connection. Apart from this, discussion on a bill in its Second Reading is unlikely to last more than two days, and this allocation of time is justified by the importance of this part of the procedure.

The Committee stage, involving detailed examination of the bill and consideration of amendments, is necessarily much the slowest. Delay at this stage may cause a blockage in the legislative 'pipeline'. This careful scrutiny, however, is designed to protect the citizen against the hardships which badly-worded legislation can inadvertently impose. Even under the present system a bill which has passed through all its stages in the House of Commons may be heavily amended still further in the House of Lords, not from party interest but simply to make the bill a workable piece of legislation. Lord Morrison has indicated, for instance, how extensive and valuable the services of the House of Lords were over some of the nationalisation bills of the 1945–51 Labour Governments. The defects which may still exist in a bill after the Committee stage do not suggest that any shortening of the time available would be desirable. It is arguable that it is the composition of the Committees which is primarily at fault. K. C. Wheare in *Government by Committee* examines the idea in some detail.[1] It is true that experts only form a proportion of Standing Committees, and that sometimes owing to the specialised nature of the bill, and to difficulties involved in the availability of M.P.s, experts are in a distinct minority. The idea has been advanced that smaller Committees, composed completely, or largely, of experts would be more appropriate. Certainly the present size of Standing Committees, consisting of 40–50 members, seems unduly cumbrous, and it might be that the experts would be less likely to be diverted from their essential business at the Committee stage than the non-specialist M.P. chosen to serve on Committees because of his party affiliations. Whether any saving in time would result is problematical, and, apart from this, there is an aversion in the House of Commons to allowing any addition to the considerable amount of national business which is already dominated by the specialist. While it is true that the party element in Committee work can lead to deliberate obstructiveness, where every detail is forced to a division by the Opposition, the Government has 'reserve' powers for using the Closure, Guillotine, and Kangaroo procedures, which can circumvent these political manoeuvres. Their use of these

[1] *Ibid.*, pp. 129–35.

closure devices is reluctant and comparatively infrequent, and on the whole preferable in the eyes of the House of Commons to giving the expert undisputed sway. Changes at the Committee stage, therefore, seem improbable. It has been suggested, however, that more use should be made of an existing procedure by which the Committee stage of bills can be taken by a Joint Committee of both Houses, after which the Report and Third Reading stages take place separately in the two Houses. This would dispense with one Committee stage of the usual process. There is no objection in principle to this, but the difficulty is that it would be impracticable to secure sufficient synchronisation of the work of the two Houses to make this procedural device applicable, except on rare occasions.

The Report and Third Reading stages also seem unlikely to be changed. The purpose of the Report stage is to make the House of Commons (or the House of Lords) aware of amendments made to the bill in Committee, and to give an opportunity to those who were not members of the Committee to add further amendments. The Government may also wish to introduce new clauses or amendments. Much of this work will be tedious, but it is necessary, both to emphasise the responsibility of the House for legislation and as an additional security against any loophole overlooked by the Committee itself. It was suggested to the Select Committee on Procedure in 1946 by Sir Gilbert Campion, himself an authority on Parliamentary procedure, that the Report stage could, with advantage, be taken from the whole House and dealt with by the Standing Committee concerned with that bill.[1] This Committee would have dealt with the Committee stage of the bill by delegation to sub-committees of its own members. The Report stage would then be signalised by these sub-committees reporting progress to the Standing Committee itself. This would save the fairly lengthy time, possibly two or three days, spent in reporting amendments and discussing new ones in the whole House. The Select Committee opposed this suggestion, however, on the grounds that the gain in Parliamentary time would not compensate for the diminished influence of the whole House over amendments. Nevertheless, if any change in legislative procedure for a non-financial public bill does come about it is the Report stage which is

---

[1] For a fuller examination of Sir Gilbert Campion's proposals, and of the Reports of the Select Committees on Procedure of 1945–6 and 1958, see A. H. Hanson and H. V. Wiseman, *Parliament at Work*, Ch. II.

most likely to be affected; in practice it is clearly those who have already participated in the Committee stage who are most likely to make further contributions when the bill is reported to the whole House. If the Committee were to be given this further responsibility it would always be possible for members, if a sufficient minimum were stipulated, to ask that particular bills should be referred to the whole House for Report. The proposal appears reasonable, but the House of Commons has an understandable bias in favour of conservatism in Parliamentary affairs, since the present procedure has been devised from long experience, though scarcely of conditions comparable to those of the present day. The final stage in both Houses is the Third Reading. This is usually brief, often taking place on the same day as the Report stage, and it gives the Opposition its last opportunity of stating objections before the bill passes to the other House. It would serve no useful purpose, therefore, to remove the Third Reading stage.

In general, it can be seen that there can be little expectation of shortening the legislative process for the non-financial public bill. Turning to other types of legislation it is possible that time could be saved by allowing Private Bills to be considered exclusively by Committees, instead of the present system which allows public business to be interrupted at 7.0 p.m. for the consideration of matters unlikely to be of much interest to the vast majority of M.P.s. This interruption, however, may well provide a convenient lull between the two halves of a debate, and apart from this, Private Bill legislation has become much more rare, having been partly superseded by the issue of Government Department Orders; moreover, if a Private Bill is unopposed its stages in Parliament are so formal as to be negligible in its consumption of time. In respect of other legislation, such as financial bills and Private Members' Bills, the issue is not so much how time can be saved as how the time allotted can be put to better use. Private Members' time has already been reduced compared with pre-war days, and it would be undesirable to make still further inroads. It would be advantageous, perhaps, to review the somewhat haphazard procedure of selection of Private Members' Bills by ballot, but that is another matter. In financial matters the situation is much more complex. The importance of finance makes time-saving out of place unless it leads to greater efficiency. As will be seen later, the 1958 Select Committee on Procedure made a somewhat tentative reconnaissance in that direction in its examination of the possible value of a Finance Committee of some fifty members, but it would need a much more drastic reorganisation than was suggested, and a complete change of approach by the House of Commons, to bring about any drastic saving of the time at present given to financial matters.

The Select Committee on Procedure of 1958, like its many predecessors, found that it was very difficult to secure any better use of Parliamentary time. The Committee was in no way hampered by scarcity of ideas. Among the suggestions considered were morning sittings of the House of Commons on Mondays, Wednesdays, and Fridays; the use of a specialist Colonial Affairs Committee, and of a specialist Defence Committee to consider the Estimates; use of the Standing Committees of the House for the consideration of the Report stage of most bills; the use of a Finance Committee to share the work on the Finance Bill with the House of Commons; a more even spread of Supply Days through the Parliamentary session, in recognition of the fact that Supply Days are used for general debate rather than for discussion of specific issues arising from the Estimates, and that the latter are not presented until February; the putting of questions before three Committees of the House of Commons on two days a week to reduce the pressures of the normal Question-time procedure (on Tuesdays and Thursdays, however, the existing procedure would be maintained); a reduction in the number of oral questions permissible for each member from three to two on any one day; an end of the practice by which Privy Councillors were given automatic precedence by the Speaker when more than one member rose to speak at the same time; the setting aside of one hour during major debates for five-minute speeches, and examination of various methods for reducing the time and energy lost in the division lobbies. This list of suggestions is not exhaustive but it is enough to indicate the amount of ingenuity expended.

Some of these ideas were dismissed by the Select Committee itself. Morning sittings, for instance, were rejected, partly no doubt because of the claims of other Parliamentary duties during the morning. M.P.s need to deal with correspondence, help constituents, visit Government Departments, and serve on Committees. In addition, it has been calculated that approximately 60% of M.P.s have to combine their Parliamentary work with the continuance of their private employment. This has led to recent suggestions that an increase in the salary of M.P.s, considerably in excess of the £1,750 a year they receive at present, would make unnecessary these outside business attachments, so that M.P.s could devote the whole of their attention to Parliamentary affairs. The salaries and facilities granted to M.P.s compare unfavourably with those of legislators elsewhere in the world. Securing service to the community at bargain-prices is one of our less amiable national characteristics, but it exerts such inhibiting force that M.P.s, though they have the remedy in their own hands, have been reluctant to vote for themselves a salary adequate for their needs. A second suggestion rejected by the Committee was for the adoption of the method of voting by a push-button device operated by electricity. This system has been used in Sweden and would save a good proportion of the 10–15 minutes taken up under the present procedure while M.P.s troop in and out of the division lobbies. This 'electrical' voting might be particularly useful on the last of the twenty-six Supply Days when there are many divisions as the last of the Estimates are rushed through; this procedure is physically exhausting for the older member as well as being time-consuming. There is the traditional view however, once put by Mr. Baldwin to an earlier Select Committee, that the tour of the lobbies helps passions to subside. As much of Parliamentary procedure is directed towards moderating the strong feelings of M.P.s it is not surprising perhaps that this traditional view prevailed; moreover, it is not altogether established that this system would be immune from the attentions of the practical joker.

Although the Select Committee rejected some of the suggestions made, it approved in general those which involved fuller use of Committees, reduction in the volume of oral questions, and greater opportunities for back-benchers to speak in debates. These suggestions were debated in the House of Commons on July 13th, 1959, and on February 8th, 1960, and announcements relative to the matters discussed were given at various times during this period by Mr. Butler, the Leader of the House. For a variety of reasons few changes were made. The reduction of the number of oral questions from a permissible three to two a day from each questioner won favour. On the other hand and perhaps predictably, no scheme which involved any delegation of House of Commons work by means of fuller use of Committees met with approval. The House of Commons generally shows a strong determination to keep most stages of its business in the hands of the House as a whole. The suggestion of a more even spacing of Supply Days secured general support, and sympathy was shown for the difficulties of the back-bencher. On the specific matters of five-minute speeches, and the automatic precedence of Privy Councillors in debates, the feeling was that these matters should be left to the goodwill of the House and of the Speaker. Changes, therefore, were few. There is no doubt of the innate conservatism of the parties over Parliamentary procedure, and, apart from this, the Government has to consider the possibility of its work being hampered by procedural changes which might lessen its authority.

There is one aspect of Parliamentary affairs, however, which may make far-reaching procedural changes unavoidable, if Parliament is not to be regulated to a merely subordinate role in the constitution. This is the crucial matter of the extent of Parliamentary control over national finance. The existing financial procedure has been under heavy critical attack for many years. It is not merely shortage of time which makes supervision sketchy, but also the difficulty of bringing to bear at the right time, and in the right way, the expert financial knowledge undoubtedly to be found amongst some members of the House of Commons. The present system too often condemns them to pass 'on the nod' huge sums in a manner which they would regard as intolerably inefficient in the management of their own businesses. The nationalisation of the Bank of England in 1946, followed by the abolition of the Ministry of Economic Affairs in 1947, when Sir Stafford Cripps moved to the Treasury as Chancellor of the Exchequer, placed the Treasury in a position of unchallenged supremacy over financial affairs. The secrecy which surrounds the preparation of the Budget and other aspects of economic policy has sometimes led Chancellors of the Exchequer to work with their Treasury advisers in isolation not only from M.P.s, but even from fellow-Ministers. The Governor of the Bank of England may offer advice to a Chancellor, but he is not bound to heed it. If the policies devised under the present system had been more demonstrably successful the dominance of the Treasury would be correspondingly acceptable. In fact, the 'stop-go' policies of the post-war years have caused widespread criticisms among City interests and industrialists who need stable policies giving a fair expectation of good returns from capital investment. Although Treasury influence is dominant, primarily on the grounds of the expert knowledge to be found there, its effectiveness as a planning organisation capable of forecasting the results of its actions has increasingly been called in doubt during its fluctuations in policy in recent years. This naturally has its impact on the general public as well as on business-men. The watch-dog for the general public ought to be the House of Commons itself, but a brief examination of financial procedure will show how slight is the influence which the House brings to bear.

Financial business is slight at the beginning of the Parliamentary session. There may be Supplementary Estimates to consider, if a Government Department, since the previous estimates were passed, has become involved in additional expenditure. Enterprises such as the Suez Canal attack, or, more recently, the help given to Malaysia may necessarily involve the Service Departments in unforeseen expenditure. The House of Commons sanctions the additional amount, but at this stage it is only able to discuss the sum being allocated as a Supplementary Estimate, not the general policy which made the expenditure necessary at all. Discussion, therefore, becomes largely a waste of time, since the only issue for debate is likely to be of more interest to an accountant than to an M.P. Sometimes, too, there will be Excess Votes to consider, when a Government Department has failed to calculate its requirements adequately and finds itself deficient at the end of the financial year. The sums involved are normally very small, otherwise it would be a serious reflection on the Department involved. Supplementary Estimates, therefore, are concerned with current spending and Excess Votes with the spending of the last completed financial year. In both the House of Commons is, in effect, confronted with a *fait accompli*. Even when the Excess Vote involves a large sum, as it did in 1959, when almost £95,000 extra was required for National Insurance and Family Allowances,[1] it could be claimed, with good reason in this instance, that exact forecasting of the sum required presented insuperable difficulties.

Of greater importance than these supplementary sums of money are the main estimates themselves. These are ready for examination by the House of Commons by February, and show in detail the proposed spending by Government Departments in the forthcoming year. They will already have been scrutinised very carefully by the Treasury. The Treasury will know, both from its

[1] See E. Taylor, *The House of Commons at Work*, p. 200.

records of previous departmental expenditure and from knowledge of current trends in the financial policy, which it so largely shapes itself, whether any adjustments are needed. Treasury examination, therefore, is concerned with the efficient spending of money in detail within the limits imposed by the Department's policy. This policy in turn is limited by the financial resources available and, in this, it is again the Treasury which is the final authority. In view of the Treasury's paramount influence it is understandable that serious doubts have been expressed, both inside and outside the House of Commons, as to the ability of the House to control expenditure. Debates on the estimates have a sense of unreality since members can hardly fail to be aware that potentially the most effective contributors to the debate are the Treasury officials, who are debarred from participation in it. In recognition of this fact the House on its twenty-six Supply Days shuns altogether any attempt at detailed scrutiny of the estimates; instead, the time is used at the discretion of the Opposition for general debates on the Government's administration of affairs.

Nevertheless, these debates could be a means of securing some measure of financial control if they were consistently directed towards their supposed objective of protecting the nation from wasteful policies. Relevant policy debates could be of the utmost value if they prevented the adoption of over-ambitious development plans divorced from any sense of financial reality. Although it has been said in criticism of the House of Commons that it does not scrutinise the details of expenditure, this matters much less than an adequate review of policy aims. Such a review, leading to amendments, could clearly save more of the nation's money than cutting down expenditure on a Government Department's stationery, for instance. Detailed examination of that kind could appropriately be left to the Treasury officials. The weakness of the present procedure in the House of Commons lies not so much in the lack of time for consideration of financial business as in the way debates stray away from what should be their major objective, namely the economical use of the nation's money. The responsibility for this vital matter is apt in present circumstances to lie somewhere between the House of Commons, the Treasury, and the Government; divided responsibility is notoriously unsatisfactory and productive of uncertainty.

There is undoubtedly urgent need for continuous vigilance over

Government expenditure, not only on the general grounds that it is the taxpayers' money which is being used, but also because of the great increase that there has been in recent years in Government expenditure. Between 1948 and 1958, for instance, expenditure rose by 50%. The root of the trouble is probably political, in that no party is anxious to give the impression of being niggardly over schemes for social development, but these schemes could well be nullified if they are not accompanied by financial stability. Attention has been called to this dangerous situation by Viscount Hinchingbrooke and by Mr. Peter Thorneycroft, who was himself Chancellor of the Exchequer in 1957–8.[1] They have both protested against the practice of giving formal approval to the very large sums comprising the vote on account, and then proceeding to a debate on matters which are of general national interest, such as unemployment problems, but which have little relevance to the spending of money by any particular Government Department, and still less to possible savings in Government expenditure. Even though the present procedure for the examination of financial policy may not be ideal it is still possible that better use could be made of it if purely financial considerations were given greater priority by all parties.

In April examination of the Estimates gives way temporarily to the announcement of the Budget resolutions by the Chancellor of the Exchequer. These arouse more public interest than the Estimates, but are in a sense less important, since revenue needs are obviously dictated by the requirements of Government Departments. If their proposed expenditure were suitably pruned, therefore, during the examination of the Estimates, the Budget could be made correspondingly encouraging to the taxpayer. The Budget is naturally devised in great secrecy by the Chancellor of the Exchequer and the Treasury officials to prevent speculators from gaining financial advantage. Even the Cabinet members are only told of the terms of the Budget shortly before it is disclosed to the House of Commons. Once it has been announced there are good opportunities for debate in the summer months, since the Finance Bill, in which the Budget resolutions are eventually incorporated, is regarded as 'exempted' business; this term simply means that the House can continue discussion beyond the normal time for the

[1] See A. H. Hanson and H. V. Wiseman, *Parliament at Work*, pp. 271–8.

adjournment. Modifications can be made, therefore, to Government financial policy, but speeches in so large a body as the House of Commons tend to be discursive. This led the Select Committee on Procedure of 1958 to suggest that examination of the Finance Bill should be shared between the House of Commons and a smaller Finance Committee.

The Finance Bill and the Appropriation Act (which authorises the allocation of money as the House of Commons has decided) are passed towards the end of the Parliamentary session; with their passage, scrutiny by the House of Commons, sitting as a Committee of the whole House, is ended too. There are, however, two smaller Committees, the Estimates Committee and the Public Accounts Committee, whose work also deserves consideration. At the outset it should be stated that these two Committees can only partially remedy the present incomplete supervision of national finance. The Select Committee on Estimates consists of thirty-six members. Membership is roughly in proportion to the party position in the House of Commons, so that there is an assured Government majority in the Committee, and the chairman is drawn from the Government party. This does not make its supervision nominal since there is an obvious incentive for Government supporters to be vigilant over the estimates so that charges of waste and extravagance may not be made by critics later. Besides, the chairmen of the sub-committees into which the Estimates Committee divides for the more thorough examination of proposed spending may well be from the Opposition. The Committee has the power to summon officials before it to give evidence, and to ask for written statements from departments. K. C. Wheare in *Government by Committee* has pointed out that, though the members of the Committee are laymen and do not have expert assistance of the kind the Public Accounts Committee receives through the Comptroller and Auditor-General and his staff, they are very greatly helped by the preliminary work of the Clerk of the Financial Committees.[1] This House of Commons official presents the Committee members with the information they require in a form which enables them to consider it with the maximum dispatch. Yet, when all these factors have been considered there are severe limitations to the effectiveness of the

[1] K. C. Wheare should be consulted on the work of the Select Committee on Public Accounts and the Select Committee on Estimates, Ch. VIII, *op. cit.*

Committee. There is not time in a single session for the Committee to examine all the estimates, so it merely examines a cross-section of them, preferably those for services affecting several departments. Again, the Committee has no power to alter the policies on which the estimates are based. Sometimes, as Professor Wheare has pointed out, the Committee must infringe on policy matters if it is to do its work properly. In doing so, however, it is acting outside its terms of reference with a corresponding weakening of its position. Even within its terms of reference criticisms made by the Committee against a Government Department have no overriding force, and may well be answered in firm terms by the Government Department concerned. At the same time, if Departments are willing to accept criticism, improvements can be effected by the Committee's reports. The chief value of the Committee in fact lies in the supervision of the work of the officials in the Treasury and other Government Departments; it has no power to modify a policy fundamentally since this is regarded as an infringement on the functions of Government and Parliament. A basically extravagant policy from a wider national point of view may, therefore, be put into practice with only marginal criticisms, if any, being made by the Select Committee on Estimates.

Somewhat similar considerations apply to the Public Accounts Committee, though there are differences of detail. This Committee of fifteen members has the expert help of the Comptroller and Auditor-General and his large staff. It investigates irregular or wasteful spending and is held in some awe by Department officials. Its reports have been rarely debated in the House of Commons and are for the information of the Treasury and of the Departments. The Public Accounts Committee is generally held to be in a stronger position than the Select Committee on Estimates for securing effective action. The fact that the chairman of the Public Accounts Committee is taken from the Opposition is also looked on as a source of strength, though, as was pointed out, the choice of the Estimates Committee chairman from the Government party does not mean that criticism will be any the less effective. But, whatever the opinion may be on this matter of the chairmanship, this is merely a side-issue. The essential fact remains that, like the Estimates Committee, the Public Accounts Committee is fundamentally inhibited by its terms of reference. It can only decide whether money has been spent honestly and economically in

attaining certain political objectives. The desirability of those
objectives is not itself considered. It appears, therefore, that both
in Committees of the whole House and in the subsidiary committees there is little or no attempt to relate policy proposals to the
resources available. However, there has been some effort recently
to establish a firmer connection between Parliament and these two
financial committees. On July 26th, 1960, Mr. Butler advanced
proposals, to be put into effect in the following session, by which
three days would be provided for debate on the reports from the
Estimates Committee and from the Public Accounts Committee.
Two of these days would be taken from the time allocated to
Supply Days and the other would come from Government time.
This rearrangement of time was coupled with a reorganisation of
the Estimates Committee timetable to encourage the appearance of
the Committees' reports as early as possible in the session to give
more opportunity to the House for debate upon them. Even with
these changes, the size of the House of Commons and the varying
degree of financial knowledge to be found amongst its members
make the thrifty use of resources which a large business might
show out of the question. There is naturally a strong temptation to
leave these considerations to the Treasury. There are some
matters, in fact, such as investment programmes, grants to local
government authorities, and wage negotiations, which are not discussed at all in the House of Commons as financial matters, but are
decided by the Treasury and the appropriate Minister.

The House of Commons in the past has always been keenly
conscious of its financial responsibilities. In a sense it still is, since
it is clearly most reluctant to delegate its duties over finance to any
subsidiary committee of the House itself. Yet there is the curious
contradiction that it has, in practice, delegated powers of decision
of the most vital financial importance to the Treasury in particular,
and to some extent to the nationalised industries. The chief need
within the House of Commons is for well-informed, concentrated,
and relevant criticism of policies involving large sums of public
money. This need might be partly supplied by the Finance Committee proposed by the Select Committee on Procedure appointed
in 1958. The Select Committee's proposal was a modest one, that
work on the Finance Bill should be shared between the Finance
Committee and the House of Commons; no doubt this cautious
suggestion was influenced by the general antipathy of the House of

Commons towards giving any measure of authority to its committees. Though it may appear paradoxical, the House of Commons would strengthen its position by greater delegation of its powers to a strongly composed Parliamentary committee. This would create a useful counterbalance to the dominance of the Treasury. Its membership would present no great difficulty. Its size would be small, certainly no more than 50, though it could not be much less because of the need to form sub-committees. In a House of 630 members it would not be difficult to find M.P.s with sufficient financial acumen to make their services valuable in such a committee. At present, the House of Commons does itself less than justice on financial matters, since those members with the requisite knowledge are unable to bring it to bear effectively under the present procedure. Although there is a prejudice against specialist committees in this country on the grounds that they may become too self-important and hamper the work of the Minister and his Department, there is also the constitutionally vital doctrine to consider of the need for full accountability to the Legislature for the actions of the Executive. In respect of the important matter of finance this accountability at the moment is little more than a pretence.

A specialist financial Committee, sufficiently expertly composed, could reinforce very strongly control of the Executive by the Legislature. Its main concern should be the Estimates but it should be a much stronger body than the Estimates Committee, which it could supersede. It would need to be able to summon officials, mainly to elicit information, and it would be desirable for Ministers, or junior Ministers, to explain the financial implications of their policy proposals to the Committee. Emphasis should be on the study of policy rather than on small-scale detail since it is policy amendment which gives greater opportunities for saving; moreover, the Treasury is vigilant over expenditure in detail. Obviously there may be times when haggling over policy expenditure is inappropriate, but rather more haggling over Government expenditure since 1945 might well have been welcomed both by the general public and by M.P.s themselves. There is a difficulty to be faced over the party composition of a Finance Committee. This should be in proportion to party strengths in the House of Commons, though the chairman could come from the Opposition. This composition may lead to mechanical acceptance of Government proposals. On the other hand, Government back-benchers have frequently been critical of Government spending in recent years and party loyalties would not necessarily blind specialists, particularly, to the need for desirable economies. Apart from this, Opposition members who served on the Committee could gain invaluable information from Ministers, officials, and their own observation; this would canalise debate on Supply Days much more effectively than happens at the moment. Greater concentration on purely financial issues would avoid waste of Parliamentary time and of the taxpayers' money. It would also make it easier to ensure that the expert advice on estimates and public accounts, available admittedly under the present system but used too little and too belatedly, would be taken much more fully into account. While it would be undesirable to give the Finance Committee any power of decision its reports could be debated in the House of Commons. Since it would have more influence than the present Estimates Committee, and a wider range of work, its reports would be more likely to attract attention. Besides, its mere existence would constitute a more effective restraint on Executive control of finance than exists so far. Critics will have their own views on where money might have been saved in recent years, but, as an instance, expenditure on missile construction would seem to rank high among projects where closer Parliamentary surveillance might have saved money.

Both the problems considered in this chapter — the time available for Parliamentary proceedings, and control of national finance — raise issues touching on the essential purposes of the House of Commons. Neither of these problems is insoluble. A greater willingness to delegate work to its own committees and a greater confidence in its own latent powers would do much to remedy some of the present-day weaknesses. Confidence in its powers is not helped by the fashionable cynicism prevalent among the public towards politicians, nor by excessive preoccupation with party warfare in debates. It serves little purpose to be a member of an historic institution unless it leads to a full awareness of the significance of that history. The historic objective of the House of Commons, since the seventeenth century, has been to protect the community against misuse of power by the Executive. This is the responsibility of the whole House of Commons, irrespective of party. There is ample evidence that many M.P.s are keenly aware of this responsibility. Yet there is no doubt that, if party allegiances were to become too rigid, the House of Commons would not be able to fulfil its historic role. This is of considerable relevance to the future development of Parliamentary procedure. If procedural reforms were habitually to be considered merely from the standpoint of securing a position of advantage which would help one or other party to win the next election it is abundantly clear that this could be a serious obstacle to national interests.

FURTHER READING

Lord Campion, *An Introduction to the Procedure of the House of Commons* (Macmillan, 3rd Edition, 1958).

Eric Taylor, *The House of Commons at Work* (Pelican Books, 5th Edition, 1963).

A. H. Hanson and H. V. Wiseman, *Parliament at Work* (Stevens, 1962).

Peter Richards, *Honourable Members* (Faber, 1959).

K. C. Wheare, *Government by Committee* (Oxford — Clarendon Press, 2nd Edition, 1955).

B. Chubb, *The Control of National Expenditure* (O.U.P., 1952).

P. Einzig, *The Control of the Purse* (Secker & Warburg, 1959).

7

Voting Systems

Characteristics of the British voting system. Other systems:
cumulative voting, party lists, second ballot, alternative vote,
single transferable vote. Merits of proportional representation.
Reasons why it has not been adopted. Assessment of the possible
effects if post-war elections had been by proportional representation. Retention of the existing system coupled with the emergence of a single reforming party would give the best solution.

THEME: No voting system combines fair representation with the
certainty of stable government. The existing system works best
when there are only two parties, but, even in the present situation,
it is preferable to the alternatives.

Voting, as it is conducted in Britain, is looked upon as the
climax of the democratic process. Because of its quasi-
sacrosanct nature it merits rather more attention than it is
sometimes given. The freedom of the voter to use his vote as he
chooses, or not at all, is a feature of the system which can be taken
for granted. Apart from this, the usual defence of the British
method of voting is that it is simple, expedient, and, by and large,
fair. The least controversial aspect of the system is its simplicity.
All British subjects over the age of twenty-one are allowed to vote,
with certain self-evident exceptions such as peers, lunatics, and
various categories of law-breakers. On the appointed and well-
publicised day the voter merely has to go to the polling-station and
place a cross on the ballot-paper against the name of the candidate
he favours. The choice will generally lie between two or three
candidates; it would be unusual for there to be more than four
candidates. The system needs little understanding, and the number
of spoilt ballot papers is negligible.

The simplicity of the system is easy to establish, but the claim of
its expediency is another matter. It is said to provide a stable
government since it favours a two-party system. The party forming

the Government will have a working majority, and the other party will form a strong opposition, ready at the shortest notice to take over if internal divisions should bring about the downfall of the Government. The suggestion that the British system of voting encourages the two-party system is probably true. The 1920s provide some exceptions, but this was a period when the challenge to Conservatism was being taken over from the Liberals by the Labour Party. This produced situations such as the election of December, 1923, when Britain experienced in an extreme form difficulties imposed by a three-party system. The Conservatives gained 256 seats, Labour 191, and the Liberals 158. The two latter parties combined to defeat the Conservatives in January, 1924, when Parliament met, and the Labour Party came to power as a minority government. The near equality between the three parties did not last. By 1929 when the Labour Party formed its second Government Liberal representation had shrunk to 58 seats, the Conservatives had 260, and the Labour Party itself 288. The Labour Government was still a minority one, but the pattern emerges of one radical party being squeezed slowly but decisively out of prominence while another takes its place. Supporters of the British system look on the situation in the 1920s as a purely temporary phenomenon, therefore, but it should be realised that it may recur if there should be a revival of Liberalism. A repetition of the election results experienced in the 1920s might then be expected, though there is no certainty that it would resolve itself as quickly as it did then by the virtual disappearance of one of the radical parties.

The British electoral method may not automatically produce a two-party system, but the elections of this century, with the exception just mentioned, show that it tends to do so. Experience of the three-party system in the 1920s, producing two minority governments, established an understandable preference in Britain for the two-party system. Coalitions in Britain in the twentieth century have not been notably popular, excluding war-time when a common objective unites the parties. The coalition of 1918–22 of Liberals and Conservatives under Lloyd George's leadership developed such strains that it broke down. The National Government of 1931 began as an all-party government, but in the House of Commons, and eventually in the Cabinet, the Conservatives were so preponderant that it hardly qualifies for the description of a coalition. Coalitions then, whether voluntary as in 1918, or involuntary as in the 'Lib.-Lab.' alliance of 1924, have not been associated with stable government in Britain. The advantage claimed for the system that it makes coalitions unlikely is therefore an important one.

Since the inter-war years could perhaps be regarded as a period when the Liberal Party was giving way to the Labour Party it would be fairer to consider the working of the system in the post-1945 period. Advocates of the system would no doubt agree that the situation had then stabilised itself with the virtual disappearance of the Liberal Party. Three elections, those of 1945, 1955, and 1959, created governments with substantial majorities, so that there was no need to consider even the possibility of a coalition. Two of the elections, however, gave very narrow majorities indeed to the Labour and Conservative Parties respectively. In 1950 Labour had 315 seats, Conservatives 297, and the Liberals 9. In 1951 the Conservatives had 320, Labour 296, and the Liberals 6. Even when the third party has been reduced to numbers which are artificially small in relation to its general support in the country, it is obviously still quite possible under the British system to obtain a result where the Government majority is very precarious. Furthermore, had the Liberals gained only a few more seats they would have been in a position to hold the balance between the two parties, and to select whichever party they chose to form a Government with Liberal support. The Liberal revival of the early 1960s makes it possible that what nearly happened in 1950 and 1951 could happen in the future. The weakness of the system is that it is based on the assumption that a two-party system meets the needs of the great bulk of the electorate. With only two parties to choose from the existing method is ideal, but the third party is a distinct embarrassment to the system, and the difficulty it poses has not yet been solved.

The strongest claim made for the British method of voting is that it is expedient since it leads to the formation of stable governments. This is held to justify some of the imperfections in the system which will be examined later. Yet, as has been seen, the evidence in favour of the present system is inconclusive. Even if the transition period of the 1920s is ignored on the assumption, probably fallacious, that the Liberal challenge was then ending, the post-1945 elections have produced one government in 1950 which could not stay the course, and another in 1951 which could have been ended by a very slight alteration in the number of seats gained by the respective parties.

The charge against the present system that it is unfair is based on the large number of votes which in one way or another are ignored. In industrial areas a Labour candidate may easily have a surplus of some 20,000 votes over his nearest rival. These surplus votes are wasted. Conservative majorities tend to be smaller, so that a situation can eventuate in which the Conservative Party wins more seats than the Labour Party, but has fewer total votes. This happened in the 1951 election. The Conservatives polled 200,000 fewer votes than Labour but gained twenty-four more seats. The anti-Conservative vote, taking the Liberals into account also, was 920,000 more than the Conservative vote. These figures do not fully represent the situation. The anti-Conservative vote, for instance, does not take into account the fact that party bargains were made in some constituencies so that by agreement some Conservative voters would support Liberal or Independent candidates; nor does it allow for the fact that the Labour Party did not contest some Ulster seats so that vast Tory majorities were not counted in these figures. A full assessment taking factors of this kind into acount would show some reduction in the anti-Conservative vote. Clearly, too, the trend was in favour of the Conservatives and their supporters who increased their vote by 1,225,000 approximately compared with the 1950 election, while the corresponding Labour increase was 635,000. It is relevant in this connection to realise that the 1950 election, which was rather more favourable to Labour, had only secured a very slender majority for that party, insufficient in fact to make the survival of the Labour Government possible. It may, therefore, have been sound politically that the Conservatives took office. The fact remains that by the workings of our electoral system it became possible for a minority government representing less than half the number of those who voted to stay in power until it sought re-election in 1955.

There is nothing freakish, historically, about this situation. Governments representing less than half of the voters are commonplace in recent times. In 1959, when the Conservatives had an overall majority of 100, they polled only 49·4% of the votes recorded. Between elections the swing of public opinion against the Government intensifies, as by-elections show. For most of its life, therefore, a Government will have the support of considerably less than half of the voting population. This comes about not only through the wastage of votes, where an Opposition candidate has a large majority, but also through the large number of seats which are won on a minority vote. Peter Richards, in *Honourable Members*, quotes a perfect example of this from the 1945 General Election result in the constituency of Caithness and Sutherland.[1] The figures were:

E. L. Gandar Dower (Con.)	5,564
R. McInnes (Lab.)	5,558
Rt. Hon. Sir A. Sinclair (Lib.)	5,503
Conservative majority	6

Approximately 66% of the voters were opposed to the candidate who was returned to Westminster as their representative. The existence of the third party in this century has made similar situations commonplace, even if not quite to the same degree as in the Caithness election. In 1951, and 1955, 6% of M.P.s were elected on a minority vote, but this has been the lowest figure in post-war years. In 1945 the number was 28%, in 1950, 30%, and in 1959, 13%. These figures demonstrate the unrepresentative nature of the present system. They can be justified only if it produces a more stable government than any other voting system. This is, admittedly, a powerful consideration. Its claims to do so, as has been pointed out, are not invincible. It remains to be seen whether any of the alternative voting schemes offers a better solution.

Some of these systems are unlikely to win much favour in Britain, either because of intrinsic defects or because they are so alien to our tradition. Cumulative voting, for instance, which would require large multi-member constituencies, allows each elector to have as many votes as there are seats. The voter can give all his votes to one candidate or can distribute them amongst candidates according to his preference. It is possible that minority parties would gain by this system. The larger parties would presumably put up two or three candidates for each constituency. Their supporters would be tempted to share out their votes. A small party, on the other hand, would only put up one candidate, who would gain by the fact that his supporters, with no divided

[1] *Ibid.*, p. 36.

allegiance, would give all their votes to him. This might be circumvented by systematic organisation of the voters by the large parties,
but the complexity of the scheme, coupled with its undue partiality
for minority parties, makes it altogether undesirable.

Another suggestion is the party-list system. If frequency of use
were any criterion of the merit of a voting system this would be the
best of all, judging by Continental example. Apart from Eastern
Europe it has been used in Germany, Italy, Belgium, Greece, and
France, for instance, in one form or another. It is a form of proportional representation. Multi-member constituencies are usual.
The parties each draw up a list of candidates and the elector votes
for the particular list he prefers. Seats are then allocated to the
parties in proportion to the number of votes obtained. The parties
then fill the seats from their lists by choosing their candidates in
order. Sometimes this order has been decided by the party
organisations themselves; sometimes the electors may vary the
order of the party list according to their personal preference for
candidates. The latter method involves considerable complications.
On the other hand, selection by the party organisations alone suggests a remoteness from local feeling which would not be acceptable
in Britain. A similar objection would no doubt be felt to the large
multi-member constituencies. Selection of suitable candidates by
the central party organisations does admittedly take place in
Britain, but it is apt to be unpopular locally as the 1962 by-election
in Orpington proved.[1] There is the further objection to the party-
list system that it is firmly associated in the minds of many with
election proceedings in totalitarian countries with single-party
systems.

Two other schemes, the second ballot and the alternative vote,
used in single-member constituencies, are very similar to each
other. The aim of both of these is to eliminate the winning of seats
by a minority vote, which bedevils the British system. The second
ballot, as the name implies, may require two elections. If no candidate has an overall majority at the first election the last candidate is
then withdrawn and the voters proceed to the polls a second time,
when a final decision is reached. In a country where there are

---

[1] In this constituency, traditionally Conservative, the local candidate,
Mr. Lubbock, a Liberal, decisively defeated Mr. Goldman, who was
chosen as the Conservative Party candidate primarily because of his services to Conservatism at their national headquarters.

virtually only three parties this seems a pre-eminently fair system. A possible result in a first ballot might be as follows:

Con.	25,000
Lab.	20,000
Lib.	10,000

Since the Conservative candidate has no overall majority a second ballot would then become necessary. The Liberal candidate would accordingly be withdrawn, and after much canvassing for the floating 10,000 votes, a second ballot might give the following result:

Lab.	28,000 (8,000 from the Liberals)
Con.	27,000 (2,000 from the Liberals)

The Labour candidate would then be declared elected. This system would greatly reduce the likelihood of minority victories in elections; it would increase support for the third party, in this country the Liberals, since potential supporters of the Liberals would see more hope of their votes counting. The defect in the system, which became apparent when it was used in France, was that the delay between one ballot and another led to intrigues and party-bargains in order to catch the floating vote. Apart from this there is the expense and interference with normal routine involved in a second election.

A simple way of overcoming these last objections is to use the alternative vote system. The principle is the same as the second ballot, but only one election is necessary. The voter shows on the ballot paper his first and second choices, simply by putting the figures '1' and '2' against the names of candidates. If no candidate has an overall majority of first preferences the last candidate is withdrawn. The second preferences of his supporters are then examined and allocated to the other parties. This is a simple system and fair to the three main parties, if not to the very small minority parties. The effect it would have on government in Britain will be examined shortly, after considering a further scheme which is the logical extension of the alternative vote method, namely the single transferable vote system.

The aim of this latter system is to remove completely all the inequalities of the single-ballot system. Large constituencies, returning possibly four or five members, would be necessary. There would be several candidates. Voters would show their preference, as in the alternative vote system, by putting a figure '1' opposite their first choice and '2' opposite their second choice, but then they would continue to show their preferences in order until they came down to candidates whom they felt they could not possibly support. Thus voters might return ballot papers showing as many as six or seven preferences in descending order of popularity. The next stages concern the electoral officials. They have to determine first of all the 'quota'. This is the necessary minimum number of votes required in order to secure election. To determine the quota presents no great difficulty. In a constituency of 90,000 voters, for instance, where there are five candidates contesting for two vacancies, the minimum number of votes required to ensure election would be 30,001; (this number is secured by dividing the number of voters (90,000) by one more than the number of vacancies (2) i.e. divide by 3. To this result (30,000) simply add 1.

A count of the first preferences of voters will then establish which candidates have secured their quota. Any votes they secure beyond this number are superfluous. This obviously has some relevance to the Labour Party's complaint of the large number of votes wasted in industrial constituencies where the Labour majority may be very large. The remedy for this in the system described is to distribute the surplus votes of successful candidates in accordance with the second preferences shown on their ballot papers. If 40,000 is the quota, and the successful Labour candidate has 50,000 first preference votes, then 10,000 of these are spare. The 50,000 votes are then examined for the second preferences shown. These second preferences could be in the ratio of 4:1 for the second Labour candidate and for a Liberal candidate respectively. The 10,000 surplus votes are accordingly distributed in the same ratio. Thus 8,000 would go to the second Labour candidate and 2,000 to the Liberal candidate. These additional votes may be enough to bring one or both of them up to the necessary quota, so that those successful could then be declared elected.

In a multi-member constituency there may still be additional seats to be filled. In order to give other candidates the requisite quota to ensure election the candidates at the bottom of the list are eliminated in turn. The second preferences shown on their voting-papers are examined, and distributed as the papers indicate. This will continue until all the vacant seats have been filled. If enough candidates do not obtain the quota by means of this distribution of second preferences of eliminated candidates, then third preferences are consulted and so on.

If the overriding purpose in a voting system is exact representation of the voters' wishes then the single transferable vote method is the fairest of all. There are no wasted votes, either for candidates at the top of the poll with large majorities or for candidates at the bottom of the poll who are eliminated. In both these eventualities voters know that their second preferences will be taken into account, and possibly later preferences too, so that their personal wishes will almost certainly have some bearing on the result of the election. Although the proportion of voters who actually use their right of voting at General Elections seems quite high under the present system — some 80% — this still means that many citizens do not vote. In the 1959 election seven and a half million failed to do so. Some of them would not do so whatever the system but others certainly abstain from realisation that in some constituencies their vote is likely to be wasted. The Liberals, in particular, have suffered from this feeling. Voters who would have supported the Liberals were deterred from doing so by the set-backs of the 1945–59 period. Since a Liberal victory in almost any constituency was unlikely at this time the choice for the 'floating voter' with general Liberal sympathies was either to vote without real conviction for the Conservative or Labour Parties or to abstain. The Liberal vote during these years was not entirely representative of the support which existed for them, as the by-elections of 1962 would seem to show. These successes have been brought about not by any marked change in the policy of the Liberal Party, nor in the policies of the other two parties, but simply by a change of mood, a belief that the Liberal Party is not defunct after all. Under the single transferable vote system there would have been no need for the Liberal Party to have been quite so much at the mercy of the fickle moods of public opinion. The system itself would have secured accurate representation of Liberal support. The extraneous factors which gave a false picture of Liberal support in the 1940s and 1950s would have been removed.

The features of the system which make it beneficial to the interests of the third party, at the moment the Liberals, also help other minority parties to secure fair representation. The three main parties would still be dominant under any of the suggested reforms, but it is possible that other parties could gain a few seats under the single transferable vote system. Minority parties are apt to compensate for their small numbers by their vigour and this could well lead to livelier debate in the House of Commons.

In view of the undoubted merits of the single transferable vote system it is of interest to know why it has not been adopted. A cynical answer is that no government which has come to power under the existing system would wish to court the risk of defeat at the next election by changing the system. The last Liberal Government came to an end in 1916 when a coalition was formed. The Conservative and Labour Governments since then have obviously had no motive to support a change from which the Liberal Party was by far the most likely to gain. But consideration of party advantage is not the only reason why the system has not won support. The crux of the matter is whether the single transferable vote system, or the somewhat similar alternative vote system, would provide stable government. Admittedly, stable government is not a certainty under the present system either, but the evidence suggests that there is a better chance of stability with our present method than by means of the various forms of proportional representation. These latter methods would certainly have the effect of increasing support for the Liberal Party. In 1945, for instance, Labour won 396 seats, the Conservatives 200, and the Liberals (including the Liberal Nationalists) 25. If seats had been allocated in proportion to the votes cast, and this is the idea of proportional representation, Labour would have won 307 seats, the Conservatives 256, and the Liberals 58. In fact, of course, under proportional representation the Liberal Party would be much stronger than these hypothetical figures show. Voters would no longer regard a Liberal vote as a wasted vote, and there would be many more Liberal candidates to take advantage of a system so encouraging to their interests. Even from the figures shown for the 1945 election it is obvious that if proportional representation had been used Labour would have needed Liberal support to keep the Government in being, instead of the large majority which it had in practice. In the elections which have followed it is easy to see by comparable calculations to that for the 1945 election that the effect of the system in practice would have been to give the party which came third in the polls the opportunity to place in power whichever of the other two parties it wished. No single party since 1945 would have had a working majority on its own.

It is not difficult to visualise the deadlocks, frustration, party-bargaining, compromise, and rapidly recurring elections, which would have been brought about by this situation. This, moreover, was at a critical time in world politics, when the cold war was dominating attention, when alliances were being constructed of vital strategic importance, dependent territories were seeking their freedom, plans for nuclear development and defence were being devised, while at home urgent problems of reconstruction demanded attention. The Liberal Party could hardly have accommodated itself both to the Conservative and the Labour policies over these issues; on the other hand, failure to do so would clearly have produced a deadlock on some occasions. This would have been prejudicial in the extreme to our interests, and to those of our allies. The present system may lead to the tyranny of the majority, but that is preferable to the tyranny of the minority which proportional representation is likely to produce in this country. It cannot be acceptable to put the third party with the smallest number of seats into a position where it can nominate the Government itself, merely by granting it its support. Yet the post-war voting figures show that this situation would happen more often than not if seats were proportional to the votes cast.[1]

The real need is not for a change of voting system but for a realisation that three parties are one too many. As a means of choice between two parties the British system is excellent. It is simple; it does not require large multi-member constituencies, where contact between M.P.s and their constituents is likely to be lost; it is likely to produce a Government with a sound working majority. The ideal solution, therefore, would be for the emergence of a single Radical party to oppose the Conservatives. The Conservatives represent one philosophy of government, the radicals, in their different ways, another. But the latter can hardly do themselves justice while they are divided. There has been a

[1] Employing similar calculations D. E. Butler, in the second edition of *The Electoral System in Britain since 1918*, published in September, 1963, has also pointed out the drawbacks of the system of proportional representation (pp. 189–94, *ibid.*).

movement recently towards a fusion of Labour and Liberal interests. So far it has been a failure, but there would be no better cure for the anomalies of our voting system than its success.

FURTHER READING

Enid Lakeman and J. D. Lambert, *Voting in Democracies* (Faber, 2nd Edition, 1959).
D. E. Butler, *The Electoral System in Britain since 1918* (O.U.P., 1963).

H

8

The House of Lords

Long-standing nature of the criticisms of the House of Lords. Modification of the Labour Party view of the House of Lords is significant. The use of Second Chambers in other countries. The functions and value of the Second Chamber in Britain. Attempts at reform of membership 1910–62. Reasons for the reluctance to alter the membership system.

THEME: There are anomalies in the present powers and composition of the House of Lords, but the dilemma of reconciling strong membership with limited powers has so far defied solution.

It is probable that to criticise the British constitution effectively it is necessary to be a foreigner. Only then would it be possible for the anomalies in the constitution to strike the understanding with full force. To those brought up in Britain familiarity surrounds our apparently curious constitutional habits with a haze, which we seldom attempt to penetrate. A foreigner, unfortified with our mystical certainty in the wisdom of our constitution, might well be baffled by many aspects of our system. We have a monarch who is head of all government, but with virtually no powers; we have a governing party, which, even at election-time, only occasionally represents more than half the voting population; in a democratic country we have a Prime Minister whose influence between elections is comparable to that of a dictator. Above all, we have the House of Lords still with effective powers, but with a membership qualification based on the social order of the Middle Ages.

But even in Britain, where antiquity and wisdom are so often regarded as synonymous, there have been some penetrating criticisms of the membership of the House of Lords, not least from the Lords themselves. Lord Samuel's witty remark on the composition of the House of Lords, to the effect that the efficiency of that House was secured by the almost permanent absenteeism of most of its members, was a more telling blow than the clumsier attacks sometimes aimed at the Lords. There is nothing new about these criticisms. The radicals from at least the 1870s onwards were bitterly antagonistic towards the House of Lords, and criticism rose to a crescendo over the events leading to the Parliament Act of 1911. The close association of the House of Lords with the Conservative Party was used openly by Balfour and Lord Lansdowne to achieve a degree of negative control over legislation, in spite of the huge Liberal majority in the House of Commons. The indignation of the Liberals led to the cleverly conducted political campaign between the 1909 Budget and the 1911 Parliament Act, by which the absolute veto of the House of Lords was reduced to a suspensory veto of two years, later, in 1949, reduced to one year. Among the many attacks made on the Lords in the heated atmosphere of 1909–11 the invective of Churchill, then a Liberal, stands out still with characteristic force. He called the House of Lords 'a one-sided, hereditary, unprized, unrepresentative, irresponsible absentee'.

Although the powers of the House of Lords have been greatly reduced, its composition has been little changed by the small numbers of men and women who have joined it since the 1958 Act providing for the appointment of Life Peers. Considering the violence and long continuance of the criticisms made of the membership of the Lords, it is surprising at first sight that more radical changes have not been made. The most radical change would be abolition of the House of Lords. This would show the social neatness of the guillotine, and would be based also on the apparently logical approach that as the Lords' powers have been progressively reduced in 1911 and 1949 all that remains is the completion of the process by abolishing the House altogether. It is sometimes argued that its powers are now so trivial that abolition would make little difference. For a time this outright solution commended itself to the Labour Party, and was put forward as part of their programme in the 1935 election. Experience of office between 1945–51 modified Labour opinion.[1] The Lords were able to show their usefulness by the non-partisan approach they showed to some of the nationalisation bills, where their concern was not to challenge the principle of

[1] See *Government and Parliament*, pp. 176–8, for Lord Morrison's views on the attitude of the House of Lords to the Labour Governments of this period.

the bills, but to help in making them workable in practice. So long as this approach prevailed repetition of the 1909–11 events was unlikely. The Lords may not have approved of the schemes proposed, but they were recognising the prior right of the House of Commons, as the popularly elected body, to impose its will over legislative matters.

There were some controversial issues in the Labour Party legislative programme, however, where it might have been unwise to count on the House of Lords adopting this attitude of benevolent impartiality. This applied particularly to the Iron and Steel nationalisation bill. The Labour Government was naturally anxious to make full use of its period of office, and it would have been frustrating in the extreme if its legislation of the 1948–50 period were brought to nothing by the imposition of the Lords' two-year veto, followed by a General Election which the Conservatives might win. Accordingly a bill was introduced, which became law in 1949, reducing the power of veto of the Lords to one year. Among some quarters of the Labour Party it is regarded as intolerable that the Lords should have any power of veto at all. They would like to see the Second Chamber used as an amending and advisory body, whose suggestions could be overruled if they were unwelcome in the House of Commons. There does not, however, appear to be any great pressure from any quarter for the abolition of the House of Lords. It is possible, therefore, that if many of its enemies are prepared to allow its continued existence the House of Lords may have merits to commend it. Some of these have been implicit in the description of its relationship to the Labour Governments of 1945–51, but it would now be fitting to consider more fully the arguments in favour of keeping this much-abused House.

As a beginning, it is worth realising that the existence of a Second Chamber is not unique in the Governments of the world. The existence of two Chambers in the United States, the Senate and the House of Representatives, is familiar enough, but, apart from this, bicameral government once adopted has been retained in nearly all the countries of the world. New Zealand, in 1950, and Denmark, in 1954, have abolished their Second Chambers, but these are small countries and their example is outweighed by the acceptance of the two-Chamber system in Canada, Australia, Sweden, and surprisingly, perhaps, the U.S.S.R., as well as in the

United States and Britain itself. These countries differ in the division of powers between the two Chambers. In Sweden, for instance, the two Chambers are of equal strength, and solve differences either by use of a Joint Committee, or, in respect of the Budget, by a simple majority taking the total number of votes in the two Houses combined. The urgency of Budget legislation makes this a more appropriate system than delegation to a Joint Committee. There are interesting points of difference of this kind, therefore, but it is a chastening thought for the outright abolitionists that so many of the countries of the world with a variety of political systems still find it necessary to make use of a Second Chamber, even if the membership qualifications are very different from those prevailing in Britain.

Apart from this general justification for the House of Lords there are several specific points to be made on its behalf. According to the Bryce Commission report of 1918 the chief functions of the House of Lords were to share the burden of legislation with the House of Commons, to use its power of veto to prevent over-hasty legislation, to act as a forum for debate, and to act as the final court of appeal. This last use has no relevance to the political functions of the House of Lords, and by custom only the Law Lords attend when the House is meeting in its judicial capacity. The major justification for the House of Lords is the assistance it is able to give to the Lower House in the work of legislation. Viscount Hailsham, in a recent debate, pointed out that it would be a mistake to regard the House of Lords as 'a decorative appendage'.[1] His view would command support among all the major parties. The Labour Party leaders, for instance, were far more appreciative of the usefulness of the House of Lords after 1945–51 than they had been before. The Lords during that period introduced many amendments to the complicated nationalisation acts, not primarily with any obstructive purpose, but simply to ensure the production of an efficient piece of legislation. The number of amendments made it evident that, in spite of the careful scrutiny of most legislation by the House of Commons, there is need for a vigilant Second Chamber as well. The House of Lords may also initiate

---

[1] Report of House of Lords' Debate, April 10th, 1962, col. 374. Viscount Hailsham renounced his title in 1963, and returned to the House of Commons as Mr. Quintin Hogg. It would be unfair, however, to regard this action as a contradiction of his own words.

legislation, if it is of a non-controversial nature. The Road Traffic Act of 1930, for instance, originated in the House of Lords, and its various provisions for greater safety on the roads made the Act pre-eminently a non-party measure. Obviously, public legislation of this type will be rare, but there is much wider scope for the non-party approach in private bill legislation, and in the scrutiny of provisional orders. Work of this subordinate but useful nature is ideally suited for relieving the House of Commons of some of the increasing burden of legislation. The work of acting as hand-maid to the House of Commons should, therefore, be a cause for grati-tude rather than complaint; it is essential to realise, too, that since the Parliament Act of 1911 the Lords have been shorn of the claims they unwisely made at that time to tamper with financial legislation from the Lower House.

The function of acting as a forum of debate also deserves favour-able consideration. The nucleus of regular attenders at House of Lords proceedings consists either of ex-Cabinet ministers who have earned their titles through their political work, of life peers, or of members of ancient families in whom a sense of public service is ingrained by long traditions. The presence of the latter may require more justification. Obviously there may be exceptions, but a willingness to attend House of Lords' sittings regularly is one criterion of a genuine concern for national progress; moreover, a long family record of service in national affairs ought not auto-matically to be a matter for censure. The other gibe levelled against the Lords is that many of its regular members are old to the verge of senility, a charge made on the grounds that changing economic circumstances have required younger peers to take on a full-time career. They have not the time to attend the House, and the three guineas a day expenses allowed for attendance there is no very great incentive. The creation of life peers has not greatly altered the position, since, as Lord Salisbury pointed out in a 1962 Lords' debate,[1] the life peers themselves tend to be elderly. It is admit-tedly, then, the older members who predominate, but it has yet to be demonstrated that this is harmful. Age and experience may not necessarily be interchangeable terms, but they are more likely to be so in political matters than youth and wisdom. Experience of politics and of public service provides a sound background for

---

[1] Report of House of Lords, Debate, April 10th, 1962, col. 405.

effective Parliamentary debate. These characteristics are to be found in good measure among the minority who make it their business to attend regularly. It has been asserted that the standard of debate in the House of Lords is in fact superior to that in the House of Commons, partly because of the greater experience to be found in the Upper House, and partly because party discipline weighs more lightly upon its members. Besides, without the need to placate constituents, or to win votes for the next election, peers can speak their minds freely, so that debates gain in pungency and relevance. Even the normally cursory accounts of proceedings which appear in the Press make this apparent. It is true that the House of Lords is likely to lose some of its most active members to the House of Commons following the 1963 legislation on the surrender of peerages, but hardly in sufficient numbers to weaken its debating merits greatly.

The remaining function of the House of Lords — its power to impose delay on legislation from the House of Commons — is the one which has aroused the most doubt. The power of veto has been used with great discretion since 1911. The Lords have realised that, since they have no mandate from the people, they must be content with a subordinate role in the constitution. Some Government bills have been rejected, such as the Government of Ireland Bill of 1912, the Welsh Church Bill of 1912 and the Parliament Bill of 1948. In general, however, under a Labour or a Liberal Government, the House of Lords has resorted to heavy amendments rather than rejection. During most of this time, in fact, there were Conservative Governments in power, but it can be said in defence of the Lords that, as was seen earlier in the chapter, they generally did not adopt a partisan attitude towards the Labour Government legislation of the post-1945 period. Naturally, with a Conservative majority ever available in the House of Lords, Conservative Government bills are better placed than those coming from Liberal or Labour Governments. The last time a specifically Conservative bill of major importance was rejected in the House of Lords was in 1832. This apparent partiality has called forth the defence that the Conservatives are less in need of restraint than their rivals, because Conservative reforms are unlikely to be characterised by the undue hastiness which is alleged to be the weakness of radical parties. This suggestion seems intolerable to sections of the Labour Party who feel quite able to take their own decisions on the timing and desirability of legislation. They feel that a purely nominal delay, of one month for instance, would be entirely adequate. They are on strong ground, too, in pointing out that a Labour Government is under an unfair disadvantage in that it cannot count on pushing all its measures through in its last year of office. There is always the threat that the Lords may use their power of veto though the 1949 Act has greatly reduced the effectiveness of this device. The Conservative Party, on the other hand, can bank with certainty on the help of the Lords if ever it is urgently needed.

The reform proposals put forward in approximately the last fifty years have occasionally glanced at this question of the veto, but have been much more concerned with the question of membership. The veto after all is only very occasionally applied, but the special nature of the membership of the House of Lords is much more frequently apparent. Naïve critics, ignorant of the useful functions performed by the Lords, base their attacks entirely on prejudice against any aristocratic share in the work of government. It would be foolish, however, to jettison the experience of many of the Lords simply from devotion to the ideal of levelling-down. The chief reform schemes, therefore, all take account of the valuable nucleus of knowledgeable peers, and, in their different ways, try to blend them into their new proposals.

The earliest official proposals of this century to reform the membership belong to the period of the Lords-Commons quarrel which culminated in the 1911 Parliament Act. These suggestions for reform came from the Lords themselves, but they were belated, and too closely bound up with the issues at stake at this time to be regarded as anything else but attempts by the Lords to divert attention from the crucial point, namely, which House was to have constitutional dominance. This criticism does not apply to one of the reformers, Lord Rosebery, who had made earlier attempts to reform the House's membership, but the fact that the Lords had shown little interest in these proposals until late in 1910 savoured too much of deathbed repentance. The proposals themselves are of some interest, however. They are much more open-minded than one would expect, when controversy was so heated. Lord Rosebery in November, 1910, proposed that the House should consist of 'Lords of Parliament'. Some would be elected by the peers from their own number; some would be nominated by the Crown; some would be automatically members by virtue of their office; some would be nominated by the Government, on behalf of the Crown, from distinguished members of the community who were not already in the House of Lords. This was a reasonable compromise, though the question of the number of members from each source needed to be resolved. A similar willingness to accept quite drastic modifications in membership is evident in Lord Lansdowne's proposals in 1911. One hundred members were to be elected by, and from, the peers themselves, one hundred nominated by the Crown in proportion to party strength in the House of Commons, and one hundred and twenty chosen by M.P.s organised on a regional basis. The period of appointment was to be for twelve years, with retirement at three-year intervals. The probable membership, including Princes of the Blood, Bishops, and Law Lords, would be three hundred and fifty. Both these schemes came too late and did not arouse much genuine enthusiasm in the Lords. For a time the matter remained in abeyance. The Parliament Act was duly passed, exluding Money Bills as defined by the Speaker from amendment by the House of Lords, and reducing the absolute veto to a suspensory one of two years. There were vague references in the preface to the Act to the idea of reforming the membership, but these ideas were temporarily shelved in deference to the more urgent events of the pre-1914 period.

The next reform scheme was that put forward in the Bryce Commission report in 1918. The proposals are sound enough, and recognisably similar to the Lansdowne proposals of 1911. Two hundred and forty-six members of the Second Chamber were to be elected by the House of Commons, sitting in territorial groups, and voting by proportional representation. Eighty-one peers (later reduced to thirty) were to be nominated by the Joint Committee of both Houses (five members from each); the basis of choice for them was to be their historical claims to membership. Members were to retire after twelve years, one-third being retired at four-year intervals. Again, the scheme seems a fair compromise with the selection of members weighted much more heavily in favour of choice by the House of Commons than the Lansdowne scheme. Naturally, one is left wondering why these eminently reasonable schemes were not adopted. They may be defective by ideal standards, but they clearly appear to be a great improvement on the present anomalous system. It will be seen shortly, though, that there are powerful political reasons that make it far more probable than not that any scheme for wholesale reform of the House of Lords, whatever its intrinsic merits, will be rejected.

Meanwhile, there are two much more recent proposals for reform to be considered. One of these is most ingenious. It is contained in a Fabian pamphlet 'The Privy Council as a Second Chamber'[1] by Anthony Wedgwood Benn. The author's personal objections to his own enforced transfer from the House of Commons to the House of Lords should not prevent his scheme from being considered on its own merits. The idea of using the Privy Council as a Second Chamber has several advantages. Historically, the Privy Council, from which the Cabinet once stemmed, has a strong claim to importance in the constitution. The change-over would be comparatively simple since no elections would be involved, and the Privy Council already has a Judicial Committee, expertly composed, which could take over the appellate functions of the House of Lords. The Judicial Committee is now mainly concerned with appeals from colonial and church courts, but its functions could be easily widened. The quality of the membership of the Privy Council is high; it includes, for instance, all ex-Cabinet ministers, so that the attacks made on the political inexperience of the majority of the present peers could not be levelled against Privy Councillors. There are difficulties in the scheme, since Privy Councillors may not wish to be dragooned into the Second Chamber, but these difficulties are fairly considered in the proposal. Hereditary peers, who were also Privy Councillors, would present no difficulty. They would receive a writ of summons in the normal way; so, too, would hereditary peers who were not Privy Councillors, but they would only attend on ceremonial occasions. Privy Councillors who were not in the Lords or the Commons would receive a writ of attendance. They would not be numerous, and many of them would have sufficient leisure and interest to attend a newly-constituted Second Chamber. The greatest difficulty would come in recruiting the Privy Councillors serving in the House of Commons. They would be given the power to apply for a writ of attendance to the Second Chamber if they wished — no doubt Mr. Wedgwood Benn was aware of his own similar situation in this respect at the time of writing. It is doubtful whether many would make use of this opportunity. The

[1] Fabian Tract No. 305, 1957.

main objection would be that compared to the House of Commons, the House of Lords is very much a backwater. The House of Commons is demonstrably more active and powerful. For the Privy Councillor attempting to bring his political career to a climax his presence in the House of Commons gives much better hope of advance. Such a man would be reluctant to transfer himself to the Second Chamber.

Apart from these major groups Mr. Wedgwood Benn advocates that the Prime Minister should have the power to recommend anyone else as a Privy Councillor, including women, Commonwealth statesmen, and churchmen of the various denominations. This proposal is obviously very similar to the present-day appointment of Life Peers. The appointment of churchmen from different denominations is of particular interest, since the present Church representation in the House of Lords only takes account of the Established Church, the Church of England; it is desirable to have ecclesiastical representation, but it would seem to be reasonable to allow some representation to other faiths outside the Church of England. The adherents of these other faiths are numerous; acknowledgment of their right to representation as special interest groups in the House of Lords would be in keeping with the present movement in the Church towards unity, rather than insistence on the superiority of one religion over another. There are, after all, a number of social matters, having no bearing on the establishment and ritual of the Church of England, on which archbishops and bishops rightly speak in the House of Lords. The viewpoints of the leaders of other denominations could well enrich debate.

A few special difficulties remain. Since the only Labour Governments of recent years have been those of 1945–51, there will be many fewer Labour Privy Councillors than Conservatives, while the Liberals will obviously be at a sad disadvantage. This difficulty could only be overcome by the creation of new Privy Councillors by the Prime Minister, by agreement with the leaders of the other two parties. It is improbable still that there would be anything else but a Conservative majority. This would matter less in view of the reduction in powers of the Lords also suggested in the scheme. A point of detail of some interest is that peers would have to be given the right to vote, and to stand at elections for the House of Commons, since many of them would not qualify for this newly-composed Second Chamber.

Mr. Wedgwood Benn also suggests some changes in the functions of the Second Chamber. It would be simply an advisory body with no effective power of delay. If a bill should be rejected in the Second Chamber then three months after it was sent to the Second Chamber by the House of Commons it would be put down in the latter for a fourth reading and automatically passed. Otherwise, amendments made would be reported to the House of Commons and settled by the Commons vote. The Lords would not be in a position to press amendments, therefore, as they can now. This reduction in powers of the Upper House looks as if it may be a further weak point in the suggestion. The power of delay would be so slight that it would virtually cease to matter. The present arrangement of a possible year's delay seems more reasonable. Although it is understandable that the Labour Party is concerned about the Conservative majority in the House of Lords, and this is likely to occur under this scheme too, the need for the existence in the constitution of some form of brake on hastily passed legislation is of considerable importance. The increasing burden of legislative work makes mistakes more likely. The quality of membership which this scheme would secure should lead to intelligent application of the power of the veto; it seems undesirable, therefore, to reduce it from the statutory one year to a mere three months. The unduly short veto period, coupled with the doubts about the number of Privy Councillors who could be recruited from the House of Commons, are the chief defects in an otherwise ingenious scheme.

The schemes for reform mentioned so far have mainly been of academic interest, though it can be seen that when the Government made possible the appointment of Life Peers in 1958 that idea already had a lengthy pedigree, dating back at least to the Lord Rosebery proposals at the beginning of the century. In the 1950s an idea developed which gained readier acceptance. This was for some differentiation between the regular attenders in the House of Lords, whose work there is frequently of great value to the community, and the 'backwoodsmen' for whom politics are of lesser interest. It would be unreasonable to bar the latter altogether from attending since they would then have neither voice nor vote in the country's affairs, unless they renounced their peerages. Various schemes were proposed to solve this problem. Differentiation on any permanent basis between the regular and occasional attenders would almost certainly involve a system of selection on a somewhat invidious basis; this prevented the acceptance of some of the suggestions made. Eventually it was the Lords themselves who solved the dilemma through their acceptance of a plan advanced by a committee under Lord Swinton. The essence of the plan was that at the beginning of every Parliament the Lord Chancellor should ask every peer whether he wishes to attend; if he says that he does not, or if he fails to reply, he is on his honour not to attend, and not to vote without notice. This suggestion has been incorporated in the standing orders of the House of Lords, and is a useful step towards rationalising the composition of the House of Lords.

Nevertheless, this change is only a partial reform compared with some of the far-reaching schemes previously mentioned. The point of greatest significance which emerges from a consideration of these schemes is the extreme unwillingness of governments, whether Conservative or Labour, to have anything to do with them. Since the schemes have obvious merits this attitude requires some explanation. The Conservatives are not interested in a root-and-branch reform. The Conservative peers are not quite so amenable, perhaps, to the dictates of their party leader as they were earlier in the century when Lloyd George described the House of Lords, not as the watchdog of the constitution, as it claimed, but as 'Mr. Balfour's poodle'. Nevertheless in any matter vital to the Conservative Party, support from the House of Lords would be assured. Obviously the Conservatives would not want to legislate out of existence this built-in advantage of the constitution. This does not mean that the Conservatives are opposed to all reform. Measures which would increase the efficiency and prestige of the House of Lords without unduly affecting its political balance are acceptable. A small admixture of Life Peers,[1] the use of leave of absence procedure under the present standing orders, and the payment of expense allowances are illustrations of the central Conservative purpose of enhancing the prestige of the House of Lords without forfeiting political advantage. Payment of a salary to peers, especially as an inducement to young peers to play a more active part in the House of Lords than many of them can afford to do at the moment, would be a possible extension of these Conservative ideas for re-invigorating the House of Lords without making any fundamental change.

[1] Life Peerages Act, 1958.

It might be expected that the Labour Party's desire to reform the House of Lords radically would be the stronger because of the Conservative Party's reluctance to do so. In fact, this is not so. The House of Lords, however anachronistic its composition, performs useful ancillary work in the scrutiny of legislation; the Lords know their place, constitutionally speaking; their power of veto has been drastically reduced in this century. It is still possible that a future Labour Government would further reduce the power of veto, but it would be very unlikely to amend the composition of the House of Lords very drastically. This may seem paradoxical in a party with no great respect for social divisions. The essential point, however, is that a reformed House of Lords would be a stronger House of Lords. The concentration of ability to be found there would attract much more attention to House of Lords' proceedings than it can command at the moment. Not only would the House of Commons suffer a relative decline in prestige, which it cannot afford, but the Government would be harrassed to an insupportable extent, even if the reformed House of Lords had a Government majority. To give merely one instance, it would be impossible to make Ministerial accountability to the Legislature an effective doctrine, since the Minister could not be responsible to both Houses directly, yet a strongly composed House of Lords would feel that it had claims at least as sound as those of the House of Commons to cross-examine Ministers on their policies. A far-reaching reform of the House of Lords is, therefore, unlikely. Life Peers will be created in small numbers, whether the Conservative or the Labour Party is in power, but neither party wants to create a strong House of Lords which neither would be able to control. The dilemma confronting reformers is how to strengthen the membership of the House of Lords, while at the same time denying to a reformed House the authority which the abilities of its members deserve. The present situation, for all its defects, is preferable to creating a rival to the House of Commons.

FURTHER READING

Lord Campion (Ed.), *Parliament — A Survey* (Allen & Unwin, 1963).
Martin Lindsay, *Shall We Reform The Lords?* (Falcon Press, 1948).
P. A. Bromhead, *The House of Lords and Contemporary Politics, 1911–1957* (Routledge & Kegan Paul, 1958).

9

Problems in the
Administration of Justice

Recent uneasiness over the administration of justice. An outline of criminal court procedure gives some insight into the principles of justice. Difficulties in dealing with semi-political offences. The importance of the idea of the accountability of the Government to the people. The dangers of the constitutional dependence of the Judiciary on the Executive. Suggested reforms need to be judged from the standpoint of basic principles.

THEME: The working of the British judicial system is soundly based, but its present virtual independence of the Executive should not be taken for granted.

Until very recently concern over the administration of justice was not strongly marked in the community. Those concerned with the law at close quarters knew that it was a conservative profession, that the procedure of relying on an over-worked Lord Chancellor and an understaffed Law Revision Committee for the production of reforms was unsatisfactory, and that the political parties were unlikely to be attracted to making legal reforms of little general interest to the electorate. Amongst the general public there was some concern over the high cost of civil law procedure, but on the more fundamental matter of the rights of a citizen when facing charges which might lead to the loss of his liberty or life there was a feeling, perhaps a little smug, that English justice was a model for the world. The better-informed members of the public, however, were becoming conscious of the risk of some loss in independence of the Judiciary in face of the expanding authority of the Executive. In theory the Judiciary is subservient to Parliament and, hence, in modern times to the Executive; in practice the Judiciary has for long been characterised by an impartiality which is the main reason for the high respect in which it is held. However, the peculiar circumstances of the post-war world have given national security an importance which may, in the Government's estimation, override all other considerations. The dangers are too obvious to need enumeration, but one of them manifestly is the risk that governmental pressure on judicial decisions may be more strongly felt than ever before. These feelings have crystallised in 1963 in the proceedings which stemmed from the Profumo crisis. The right of the police to detain people for questioning, the right of a defendant to be able to call any witnesses necessary to his defence, the powers of the Court of Criminal Appeal, the position of the Attorney-General who has both a quasi-judicial and a political role, have all roused controversy. Mr. Gordon Walker, the Labour spokesman, has called for a Royal Commission on the Law. As the excitement recedes, however, the events begin to drop into proportion. The best corrective to disproportionate alarm is to study the system itself, particularly the procedure in criminal law. Obviously, the system cannot be better than the people who administer it and there will be occasional individual failings for this reason. Lord MacDermott has pointed out in *Protection from Power under English Law*[1] that a sound system of law is inadequate in itself. It must be reinforced by a general sensitivity to the spirit of the law. This cannot be achieved by legislation. The primary purpose of this chapter, therefore, will be to consider the more tangible matters of judicial procedure in cases of a criminal or political nature, since these are the matters over which most concern is felt.

One of the most crucial tests of a judicial system lies in the provisions made for the treatment of the accused person from the time of the arrest onwards. A brief account of criminal law procedure, therefore, will give some insight into some of the principles which pervade the English judicial system. The outstanding feature is the thorough way in which the interests of the defendant are safeguarded. When a man is arrested he must be told what the nature of the charge is, he must be cautioned against making remarks which might be construed to his disadvantage later on, and any statement taken from him must be voluntary or else it loses its validity in court. At the earliest possible opportunity the accused must be brought to court, when the charge is stated, evidence of

---

[1] p. 41, *ibid.* See pp. 25–40, *ibid.*, for an excellent and reassuring analysis of the Attorney-General's relationship to the Executive.

arrest given, and, in the more serious cases, matters of bail and legal aid are decided. Legal aid is always given in criminal cases whenever there is the least doubt about the ability of the accused man to pay for his own defence. The privilege of being granted bail depends on the judgment of the police and the gravity of the charge, but if the defendant is remanded in custody he must be brought to court again within eight days. The purpose of this delay is simply to allow both sides to assemble evidence and witnesses. The accused will then appear again in the magistrate's court where witnesses are heard, the accused is given the opportunity to state his case or reserve his defence, and the magistrate then decides whether the prosecution has produced enough evidence to give sound reason for committal of the case to a higher court. The purpose of this procedure is, again, to safeguard the accused. If the charge against him has no substance it can be dismissed at this early stage without keeping him in custody until the time for trial in a higher court arrives. In addition, the magistrates can order that these proceedings should be conducted in private if publicity is likely to damage the rights of the defendant in a higher court. Whether private or not, Press reports of the proceedings will be purely formal so that no evidence is disclosed which might prejudice those who may be jurymen in the case later.

There may be a delay of approximately one month before the case is heard in a higher court. During this time the accused is likely to be remanded in custody. Procedure in the higher court is based on the same principles applied in the previous hearings. The accused is given every opportunity to put his case to the best advantage. He is given expert legal aid, he is allowed to produce witnesses, there are strict rules of evidence designed to protect the interests of the accused, and a summing-up by the judge to present the issues to the jury as clearly and as fairly as possible. The jurors must not be known to the accused, and he has the right, on their first appearance, to object to any number of them either because they are known to him or because they may be prejudiced, for religious or racial reasons for instance. The jury's decision must be unanimous. If the finding is one of guilt the jurors must be satisfied beyond all reasonable doubt. The accused is then sentenced, and only then is his previous criminal record, if any, taken into account. He may appeal to the Court of Criminal Appeal on matters of fact, law, or sentence. If there are special grounds for

I

doing so the Court of Criminal Appeal may allow him to appeal again to the House of Lords. It is well-known, too, that in murder cases the accused often appeals for mercy to the Queen who exercises this prerogative power through the Home Secretary.

This outline of criminal procedure has merely touched on the chief safeguards for the accused. In fuller detail there are other safeguards also, but all with the same purpose. There are occasional criticisms of the procedure. The long delay between the preliminary hearing and the hearing at the higher court has caused concern since it is possible that a man subsequently proved innocent may spend a month or more in custody before his case is fully heard. It should be remembered, however, that it will already have been established at the preliminary hearing that the prisoner has a case to answer. Furthermore, the judges whose experience best fits them for trying cases at the higher courts cannot be made instantly available to deal with one particular case out of many others. There is the alternative of allowing the accused out of custody on bail, but this will involve police surveillance and the risk of the accused escaping justice. A second criticism lies, significantly, in the fact that the defects in the procedure arise less from the fact that an innocent man may be wrongly found guilty than that a guilty man may be wrongly found innocent.[1] Most of this criticism springs from the use of the jury. The purpose in using a jury is to widen the approach to the facts of the case to embrace the ordinary man's concept of natural justice. This concept is apt to be more generous — possibly too generous — to the accused than the purely legalistic approach to guilt or innocence. If the law is out of touch with public opinion the jury is a valuable means of correction. Lord Devlin in *Trial by Jury* describes the jury as 'the lamp that shows that freedom lives'.[2] The way in which juries frequently refused to bring in a verdict of guilty in spite of the evidence in the early nineteenth century when the penal code was absurdly harsh is a well-known example of the humanity of the system. If the movement for the abolition of capital punishment gained in strength jury decisions might again be a way of forcing the amendment of the penal code. It is true, admittedly, that juries are more prone to

[1] The inability of the Court of Criminal Appeal to order a retrial, if it has to quash the verdict of a lower court on technical grounds, is an illustration of this point.

[2] *Ibid.*, p. 164.

be mistaken in their decisions than judges, but their mistakes are more likely to be in favour of the accused than against him. Besides, in trying a case it is difficult for mere human beings, whether trained or not, to be completely certain about the rightness of their decisions. It is reasonable, therefore, to weight the balance in favour of the accused.

Criminal law proceedings are clearly based on eminently sound principles which ought to apply, wherever they are appropriate, to all judicial proceedings. They give a standard by which all judicial proceedings can be judged; hence the value of knowing the procedure in some detail. The principles which ought not to be infringed without demonstrably good reason can be briefly stated. No arrest should take place without a specific charge being made both at the time of the arrest, and as soon after as possible at a public court. This would preclude the use of the 'lettre de cachet' system employed in France in pre-Revolutionary days by which men could be placed in prison without trial by purely arbitrary methods. It would not, however, preclude a dictatorial state with an entirely subordinate and docile judicial system from following these same procedures precisely in form if not in intention. There are further principles, therefore, to consider. There must be no coercion of the accused. He must be given every facility to conduct his defence effectively. This means that, even if kept in custody, he must be allowed communication with the outside world. He must be given the opportunity of receiving legal advice, paid for by the State if necessary. He must be allowed to produce witnesses who are free from any fear of victimisation. These are not principles which would commend themselves entirely to a dictatorial state anxious to secure the conviction of political opponents, for instance. But this is not all. The crucial matters of guilt and sentence, in serious offences at least, are not settled in secret by a small tribunal whose members might easily be the obedient instruments of the will of an arbitrary state. Guilt is decided by a jury of fellow-citizens chosen at random. The sentence is imposed by the judge, but there is the possibility of appeal to at least one higher court so that the sentence may be reduced or even quashed altogether. Apart from this, in a free country an unduly harsh sentence may cause a public outcry in Parliament and in the Press; knowledge of this is likely to militate against severity. Yet more important than all the points enunciated so far is the underlying principle that all procedure should be based on the presumption of the innocence of the accused. The onus of proof of guilt rests with the prosecution who must perform the task in strict accordance with rigidly prescribed rules of procedure.

It would obviously be wrong to assume that because of the soundness of the English judicial system in one respect, it is as equally effective in others. There are some offences where the courts are not so well fitted to reach a wise judgment. These are offences committed primarily for political motives. Constitutionally they are more interesting than other offences. A Government, whatever its nature, has no political interest in safeguarding or ill-using the small number of criminals in society, but it has a much closer interest in offences which spring from political differences. Political agitation with its occasional undertones of violence sets a particularly difficult problem for the courts. Since the eighteenth century Britain has been fortunate, compared with the Continental countries, to experience relatively little political disorder. When it has occurred the judicial system has been put under a heavy strain, and has operated with greater uncertainty than it does in the normal way. The disorder of the post-1815 period, the early Trade Unionist agitation leading to the Tolpuddle Martyrs case of 1834, the attempts in the 1870s to break the strike weapon by imprisonment and fines of the ringleaders, and the attempts to control the activities of the suffragettes, are instances of the peculiar difficulties confronting the courts in dealing with crimes stemming from political motives. In each of the examples mentioned the true remedy lay not in judicial action at all, but in constructive political action, such as recognition of the lawfulness of Trade Union organisation and of the right to strike.

Obviously the mere existence of agitation does not necessarily justify the demands being made. Until it has become clear whether those demands are in the national interest or not, the judges have to deal with the problems of the awkward interim period by enforcing the law as it exists at the moment. This is also difficult, partly because of the problem of deciding at what point a lawful attempt to influence Government policy has strayed over the border-line into criminal action, and partly because the Government itself is so closely concerned in cases of this kind and has special powers which may make it impossible to apply the ordinary procedure of the courts. These points have been given topical significance by the arrest of members of the Committee of One Hundred campaigning for nuclear disarmament. As part of a policy of civil disobedience actions have been carried out involving obstruction and threats to the security of Government property, in particular the aerodromes used as bases for possible nuclear operations. Apart from deciding the exact nature of the offences involved, trial by the normal procedure has been hampered by the difficulty of assessment of evidence. A full defence would necessitate a detailed examination of the rights and duties of State and citizen; it would partake more of a debate on political theory than of the normal proceedings which the courts are best fitted to conduct. It reinforces the belief, which the earlier instances quoted tend to confirm also, that court procedure is not adapted to the trial of basically political offences. Meanwhile, the judges have to do their best to protect the community with the means to hand. It needs to be pointed out also, that the present system, if not ideal, is certainly preferable to the setting up of political courts by the Executive itself, which is the probable alternative.

The other feature of the trial of these political offences which diverges from normal practice is that the Government is not obliged to state in full its case against the accused. To safeguard national interests (of which it is itself the sole judge) the Government can, on the advice of a Minister, withhold evidence which might ordinarily be considered essential for the establishment of a case. The courts have no powers to compel the Crown to produce this evidence, and accordingly have to take these aspects of the Crown's case on trust. Most people can appreciate the dilemma in which the Government is placed, since national security is an overriding interest, as the emergency powers taken in wartime illustrate. Now that the world is living in a state of half-peace, because of the tremendous speed and power of modern weapons, it is only to be expected that citizens cannot have the same freedom of action which was reasonable when war was conducted in a more leisurely manner. The new problem is to define the limits of national security. Since the Government must be judge in its own cause on this subject the situation is both difficult and potentially dangerous. The only solution is to ensure by every available means that Governments are kept as fully accountable to the people as possible.

It is still possible to secure that this idea of accountability should be applied with reasonable effectiveness. 'In a democracy,' writes Sir Ivor Jennings, in *The Law and the Constitution*, 'Government must necessarily be carried on in such a manner as to secure the active and willing consent and co-operation of the people; for a Government that fails to persuade public opinion will be overthrown at the next election'.[1] He goes on to say that the difference between a dictatorial and a free country rests, to some extent, on intangibles since 'the existence of a free system of Government creates an atmosphere of freedom which is more easily felt than analysed'. However, there are also specific principles at work in the judicial system which the general public would expect to see applied in any court case. These principles are those previously mentioned (see pages 118–22), such as the right of the defendant to state his case fully. They derive part of their strength from their long continuance. Some of them stem from statutes such as the Habeas Corpus Act of 1679. Some stem from the decisions of judges. It was the notorious Lord Chief Justice Jeffreys, for instance, so often pilloried for his harshness after the Monmouth Rebellion of 1685, who refused to accept the validity of hearsay evidence. A great deal of law and judicial procedure in England has a strong practical basis. Much of English law has been formulated as a result of innumerable decisions in individual cases. This is a better guarantee of individual rights than the phrases of a written constitution. Words change their meaning with the passage of time, so that a written constitution, however carefully devised, cannot anticipate all the circumstances which may develop in later years. Precedent, on the other hand, has a dual advantage. It makes it more obvious when a breach of customary procedure occurs; secondly, since it is not static, it can be adapted to changing circumstances without losing contact with the essential principles of justice. In brief, therefore, there are standards of conduct in judicial procedure which are generally familiar; they are not absolute and in exceptional circumstances may be infringed, but the risk of serious abuse is slight so long as Governments remain accountable to the people.

It is important to realise that these comforting reflections do not altogether preclude abuse of the judicial power by the Executive. Some of the law springs from precedents created by the judges themselves, but much of it is statutory. Statutory legislation,

[1] Sir I. Jennings, *The Law and the Constitution*, 5th Edition, p. 61.

devised by Parliament, has absolute authority in the courts. The judges may interpret statutory legislation when it is ambiguous, as they did in reaching their unexpected decision over the Taff Vale strike of 1900, but that is the limit of their authority. They cannot flout the wishes of Parliament. It was the Bill of Rights of 1689 and the Act of Settlement of 1701 which brought this about by preventing the monarch from exercising the undue judicial influence practised by James I and James II. These Acts increased the influence of Parliament. The purpose was to limit the power of the Executive. Now that modern conditions have so enlarged the power of the Executive that effective Parliamentary control is again endangered, the risk of Executive influence in the courts once more emerges as a potential, if remote, threat. What was once a security against abuse of power by the Executive could now make that abuse more easy. There is no full Separation of the Powers in Britain; the executive, legislative, and judicial functions of Government overlap, and the Judiciary is not independent; there is no Supreme Court in Britain, as there is in the United States, to nullify acts by the Executive which are a breach of the constitution; in this sense, we have no constitution. The dangers are potentially tremendous. Control of the courts is one of the first objectives of a despotic system; in Britain there would be far less technical difficulty in achieving this than in many countries which we regard as less democratic than our own.

If Parliament wished to proscribe a political party and imprison the leaders, judges who wished to retain their position would have no option but to put these laws into effect. The appointment of judges and of Justices of the Peace is by the Prime Minister and the Lord Chancellor, in practice by the latter.[1] The office of Lord Chancellor is a political appointment. He is a member of the Cabinet and has a political allegiance to it, to the Prime Minister, and to his party. This does not influence the choice of judges and Justices of the Peace at the present time, but, clearly, it could do so if a political party with little respect for precedent gained power. Political prejudice could then strongly influence appointments made, without any need at all to change the method of appointment. Dismissal of judges would present greater difficulty. By the Act of Settlement of 1701 judges may only be dismissed by a joint

[1] The Prime Minister, however, may well use his overriding authority in making the major judicial appointments.

petition to the Crown from the two Houses of Parliament. To alter this under our present constitution would require a new Act of Parliament. An intending despot would want the power of dismissal to be placed in the hands of the Executive, but oniy a Parliament far more docile than can be visualised at the moment would allow this dangerous power to pass out of its own hands. In general, however, it would not need any radical change in the present organisation of the judicial system to put it completely at the mercy of the Executive. The dangers which result can be illustrated by the political trials which have taken place in Europe and the Middle East since 1945.

In practice, the Judiciary in Britain is far more independent than a study of its organisation alone would lead one to expect. Its long history and high reputation for impartiality make it relatively safe against usurpations of its authority by the State, though, as has been seen, the formal barriers against State domination are negligible. This independence is well worth preserving. Its preservation should be a primary consideration in examining proposals for reform. It has been suggested at various times that juries should be abolished, and that Justices of the Peace should be replaced by professional magistrates. Very convincing reasons can be advanced for both these ideas. It has been suggested too that there should be a Minister of Justice.[1] This would be more clear-cut than the present system in which responsibility to Parliament for the workings of the Judiciary is shared between the Home Secretary and the Law Officers of the Government. Yet, however well-intentioned these proposals may be, each of them would make some inroad into the independence of the Judiciary; each of them would make a little easier direct control of the judicial system by the State. The abolition of the jury and of Justices of the Peace, for instance, could seal off the courts from all effective contact with the mass of the people. Verdicts given by a judge, without a jury, and the replacement of the Justices of the Peace by uniformly trained professional magistrates might lead to a more efficient system of justice, but only at the price of increasing the possibility of direct State control. It is a price not worth paying.

[1] See, for instance, R. M. Jackson's *The Machinery of Justice*, 4th Edition, pp. 381–4.

FURTHER READING

F. T. Giles, *The Criminal Law* (Pelican Books, 1963).

F. T. Giles, *The Magistrates' Courts* (Pelican Books, 1963).

L. Page, *Justice of the Peace* (Faber, 2nd Edition, 1947).

F. Milton, *In Some Authority* (Pall Mall, 1959).

Lord Devlin, *Trial by Jury* (Stevens, 1956).

A. V. Dicey, *The Law of the Constitution* (Macmillan, 10th Edition, 1959).

Sir Ivor Jennings, *The Law and the Constitution* (Univ. London Press, 5th Edition, 1959).

R. M. Jackson, *The Machinery of Justice* (C.U.P., 4th Edition, 1964).

IO

Local Government
Some Recent and Prospective Changes

The present period is one of great change. The importance of
local government to the citizen. The need for reorganisation. Why
changes are slow. The reports of the Local Government Commissions. The Royal Commission on Greater London. Probable
changes in the county structure. The effects of the block grant
system.

THEME: The present changes are overdue and are likely to
strengthen local government.

There are many controversial issues which arise from a study
of local government. In a short space only a few of them
can be considered. The issues of the greatest topical interest
are those involved in the Government's recent or prospective
legislation on the subject. Reforms affecting finance have already
been put into effect by the block grant system, imposed by the
Local Government Act of 1958, and structural changes are likely to
take place in the organisation of local government in London, and
the great conurbations of the North-East, North-West, and Midlands. These changes are not merely of importance to the authorities involved. They mark the beginning of what may eventually
prove to be a wholesale alteration in the status and powers for
many local government authorities. Nor do the changes, present
and prospective, only affect the administrators themselves. Local
government clearly involves every citizen. Police, fire brigades, and
Civil Defence services exist for his protection; the home in which
he lives may be council-owned; he is likely to have the keenest
interest in the number, variety, and efficiency of the schools in his
district; the pleasantness of the area in which he lives may be
greatly improved by an enterprising council which provides parks,
ornamental gardens, and recreational activities. These and other

services provided by the Council are under the constant close scrutiny of the citizens of that district. The quality of these services can be assessed much more readily and accurately by the citizen, from his close contact with them, than the more distant policy decisions of the central Government. For this reason alone then, changes in local government, which may affect the efficiency of the services provided, are of interest to every citizen.

There are other factors, too, to be borne in mind in assessing the wisdom of changes. For most people local government means paying rates and receiving services. Fortunately, there are many thousands of citizens about the country who also give services. These are the councillors. Motives for becoming a councillor are no doubt very mixed. A keen sense of social service, a desire for prestige, the use of local politics as a preparation for an eventual Parliamentary career, may all play their part for different people. Yet, whatever the motives, local government service itself is the same for all in that it closely associates large numbers of people with the business of government. The desirability of doing so in a democracy is obviously very great. It is of value not only to the councillors themselves, but to the whole community, since it touches on the fundamental issue of the relationship of the central Government to the citizen. Local government, with the voluntary element preponderant (for councillors receive no salary), is potentially a very strong barrier against domination of the community by central Government. The power of the latter in local affairs has increased in this century, but the limits of central control are closely defined and any infringement would be very obvious to councillors, and to the Opposition in the House of Commons. The changes proposed in the structure of local government have brought to the fore this question of the central–local relationship; with the whole system likely to be in a state of flux for some time to come it is worth being clear about the essential features which ought to be preserved.

That some changes are necessary is indisputable. The organisation of local government in England and Wales would give a wonderful opportunity to the tidy-minded administrator to display all his talents, for the system is both anomalous and anachronistic. There are far too many small authorities whose boundaries have been fixed neither by convenience nor logic. The Local Government Boundary Commission reports of 1946–7 showed what huge discrepancies in size there were between local government authorities of the same status. A County Council may be large, like Lancashire or Middlesex, each serving a population of over two million; on the other hand, it may be extremely small, like Rutland with a population of 23,000, or Westmorland with 64,000. A County Borough may, like Birmingham, have a population of one million, or it may, like Canterbury, have a population of 30,000. Yet the desirable status of County Borough, with complete independence from the County Council, has been denied to a Borough as large as Ilford with a population of 180,000. In all there are fifteen non-County Boroughs of over 100,000 inhabitants in England and one, Rhondda, in Wales. At the other end of the scale are tiny Boroughs, such as those which cluster round the Kent coast: Lydd with 3,000 inhabitants, Rye with 4,500, and New Romney with 2,500. The same discrepancies can be seen in the size of Urban District Councils. Lynton in Devon has a population of 2,000; Thurrock in Essex has 107,000; both are Urban District Councils. In fact, a change in status from Urban District Council to Borough does not matter greatly, since their powers are virtually the same, but the independence given by county borough status is of the greatest importance.

The teeming population of Greater London poses special problems. Most of the growth is taking place outside central London where, in all except a very few Boroughs, population has been falling since 1931. A glimpse of the nature of the problem can be seen in the fact that the City of London, the square mile at the centre, has about 5,000 permanent householders, but a daytime business population of 500,000. Huge dormitory towns have grown up on the outskirts of London to accommodate the great masses of London workers. Several of these towns have sufficient resources to be County Boroughs in their own right, but only three London area authorities, West Ham, East Ham, and Croydon, have this status. Some of this large area is administered by the London County Council whose constituents number over 3 million out of the 8 million population of Greater London. The remaining 5 million inhabitants have their local services administered through the Home Counties of Surrey, Kent, Essex, and Middlesex, except for the County Boroughs previously named. The present division of responsibility is thoroughly unsatisfactory as the report of the Royal Commission on Greater London made very plain.

Problems of local government administration in the area have very much in common. The present splintering of authority outside the L.C.C. area causes too parochial an approach, which is obviously inefficient for a service such as roads, where an overriding planning authority is needed for the whole area.

The illogicalities of the present system, both in London and elsewhere, spring from a failure to adapt the organisation to the needs of modern times. The present-day administrative areas of the County Councils are largely the same as those which were set up at the time of the Norman Conquest. A tract of land which could be conveniently controlled by a Norman sheriff is not automatically going to be ideal administratively for the provision of an efficient fire service, nor for coherent development of a road system suited to modern traffic. Even in 1888, when the County Councils and County Boroughs were set up by the Local Government Act, it was a little doubtful whether the existing county divisions were entirely suitable for all the services provided. Since then the local authorities have taken on new responsibilities for education, the Welfare State has been created, leading among other things to a great variety of health services, there have been large movements of population to London and the South-East, services such as gas and electricity are administered by nationalised boards, and modern improvements in transport have made nonsense of boundaries appropriate to the days of the horse and carriage.

In spite of these vast social changes, the essential framework of local government has remained unchanged throughout the twentieth century. The last major structural change was in 1899 when the London Metropolitan Boroughs were set up. Urban and Rural District Councils had been set up previously in 1894, while Boroughs and Parishes have a much more ancient history. Even within the system detailed changes have been few. Several County Boroughs were created between 1888 and 1926 but since then the system has ossified. The County Councils, with their huge variations in size, are virtually the same as they were in 1888. The immobility of the system may seem curious but opposition to any change is bound to be strenuous. The problem is not simply one of attaining administrative neatness. Local government is an important arena in party politics. Only a peculiarly altruistic Government would pioneer a scheme for a revision of boundaries from which it is likely to lose politically. Besides this, local pride seems to be felt in inverse proportion to the size of the area so that schemes for amalgamation which seem desirable administratively are likely to stir up a hornet's nest of protest from the small authorities. In these circumstances the reluctance of governments to interfere with the present structure becomes understandable.

Amongst the larger authorities the practical obstacle to a change of status is finance. This is most apparent in the way in which large Boroughs such as Ilford, Luton, and Ealing have been frustrated for so long in their attempt to gain County Borough status. In a county such as Bedfordshire the grant of County Borough status to Luton would remove at one blow a very large proportion of the rate revenue for the whole county. The standard of services in the rest of the county is likely to suffer, in spite of the likelihood of additional Government grants. Thus Luton, with a population of 140,000, that is 40,000 more than the prescribed minimum for County Borough status, has been heavily penalised under the present system. In the neighbouring county of Cambridge there is a similar difficulty. The city of Cambridge, only just short of the 100,000 suggested for County Borough status, has a greater population than the whole of the rest of the county put together. The Cambridge householder, therefore, depends for many of his services on a County Council which, in proportion to the relative populations inside the city and outside it, is insufficiently representative of his interests.

These problems have been well known for years, but action to remedy them has been slow, for the reasons previously given. A Local Government Boundary Commission investigated the situation in 1946-7 and made radical suggestions for recasting the present structure, but alarm at the likely reaction of local opinion prevented these proposals from being put into effect. In 1958, under the Local Government Act, Commissions were set up for England and Wales. The first duty of these Commissions has been to examine what changes are necessitated by the shift of population to the large conurbations. In England this has involved detailed consideration of five Special Review areas, the West Midlands, Tyneside, Merseyside, S.E. Lancashire and W. Yorkshire. The proposals on the West Midlands and Tyneside give some insight into the likely pattern of local government, since the problems of all these areas are very similar. Towns have spilled over their old boundaries and coalesced, so that the divisions have become purely arbitrary. At the moment local government services are largely provided by the County Councils whose areas these conurbations happen to overlap — in Tyneside, the County Councils of Northumberland and Durham, for instance. These Councils have the strangely mixed responsibility of looking after rural areas, small towns, and sections of the swollen urban communities. The first step suggested is the removal of these communities from the control of the present County Councils; in their place the ideal arrangement would seem to be a directly elected central planning authority for the whole conurbation, using the subordinate local authorities as agents. These local authorities would be entirely responsible for the type of service now performed by the non-County Boroughs, but greater independence than this would be likely to prejudice unified development of the area. The recommendations of the Commission make this partly possible in Tyneside where it is suggested that there should be four County Boroughs, Newcastle, Gateshead, Tynemouth, and South Shields, all included in a new Tyneside county. In the West Midlands, on the other hand, the conurbation is to be split between six County Boroughs, Wolverhampton, Walsall, Dudley, West Bromwich, Smethwick, and Birmingham, but there is no mention of a county authority. These proposals then, although an improvement on the present arrangement, still do not seem to allow fully enough for large-scale planning of the conurbations. The creation of a strong overall planning authority would undoubtedly diminish the powers of the smaller local authorities, but this need not be un-democratic in the least, rather the reverse. Apart from London, the population figures in these areas do not differ markedly from those in the larger County Councils today, so that the size itself would be no new problem; the planning authority would be directly elected, so that councillors would be conscious of their responsibility to their constituents; finally, the fact that services are likely to be more efficiently managed under this unified control would make any interference by the central Government less justified.

The Commission on Wales published its draft proposals in 1961. The interest of its proposals lies in the fact that they are planned for the whole country of Wales and, therefore, may well be a precursor of the arrangement to be expected in England when the areas other than conurbations are reorganised. The proposals are that the existing thirteen Welsh counties should be abolished and replaced by five large administrative areas, North-West, South-West, North-East, and South-East Wales, and Glamorgan. The general pattern is for a richer county to form the nucleus of each area, which would also include a few of the poorer counties to be propped up by the support of their richer neighbour. Since some of the counties of Central Wales are extremely poor this scheme has obvious benefits for them. The scheme looks sound, at first sight, but it is attempting to go to its objective too quickly. The urgency for reconstruction of the Welsh system is possibly less great than it is in the densely populated English conurbations, and this will give added force to the usual objections based on local feeling. The Welsh are strongly conscious of their history so that they can hardly be expected to take kindly to the new administrative areas with highly unimaginative names. The Fabian slogan of 'the inevitability of gradualism' could very well be applied to changes in local government structure where there is no desperate urgency.

Greater London was not included in the Special Review areas designated in the 1958 Local Government Act for investigation by the Local Government Commissions. Instead, its problems were examined by a Royal Commission under the Chairmanship of Sir Edwin Herbert.[1] The Government believed that changes in the structure of local government in Greater London were urgent. This has been challenged and controversy has centred also on the form the changes should take. The first need, according to the Commission, was to achieve unity of control for the whole of the Greater London area by the creation of a planning authority with overriding powers for the provision of the main local government services. The present boundaries of the London County Council date back to the nineteenth century. More of the inhabitants of the Greater London area live outside the L.C.C. boundaries than within, so that in its existing form the L.C.C. could not give the unity of direction required for the whole area. To provide this unity of direction the Commission proposed the setting up of a Greater London Council, directly elected, to be responsible for such services as education, traffic, town planning, and fire and ambulance services. This Council would replace the L.C.C. which accordingly, together with the Middlesex C.C., would be abolished. The Government's acceptance of the abolition of the Labour-

[1] Report of the Royal Commission on local government in Greater London (Cmnd. 1164. H.M.S.O.).

controlled L.C.C. has been criticised as a political manoeuvre, but it is fair to point out that the setting up of a larger authority is in keeping with the general movement towards larger authorities and greater unity of control visible in the proposals for the other conurbations in England. Another objection has naturally come from the counties such as Surrey, Kent, Essex, and Hertfordshire, which will lose prosperous rate-producing areas under the new scheme. The Commission stated that these counties would still remain financially viable, but it is too early to assess the financial situation accurately. Apart from these great structural changes a new valuation of rateable property in the country generally has recently taken place and there is also the possibility that the Government may give compensation to the areas suffering financial loss as the White Paper (Cmnd. 1562. H.M.S.O.) makes clear. It needs to be remembered also that financial arrangements should be determined by structure, not the reverse. It is easier and better to adapt financial organisation than it is to be saddled with an out-dated administrative structure for the provision of local government services.

The Government, itself, has raised one objection to the Commission's proposals on the functions of the Greater London Council. The Commission proposed that the Council should be responsible for education in the whole area with help from newly created Greater London Boroughs. Education, like some of the other services, suffers from the splintering of responsibility in the present system. The L.C.C. is organised into large divisions for education of up to half a million inhabitants. Yet adjoining the L.C.C. boundary there are, for contrast, two divisional executives, one, Penge, serving a population of 25,000, and another, North Central Surrey, serving a population of 203,000.[1] Variations of this kind are numerous. The Government, while accepting the need for reorganisation, has baulked at the idea of giving overall responsibility for the whole area to a single council.[2] Their suggestion is that there should be a single education authority in central London serving a population of some two million inhabitants. Outside this area the Greater London Boroughs should act as the education authorities for their own areas. The large authority in central

---

[1] These figures are taken from an article 'The Government of London' in *The Times Educational Supplement* of May 15th, 1959.
[2] Cmnd. 1562. H.M.S.O. paragraphs 38–44.

K

London will continue to make possible the freedom of choice of schools for pupils which has been taken for granted there for years. How effectively the Government's scheme for making education a Borough service will work is a matter of conjecture. It will certainly remove some of the oddities of the present system, which are imposed by purely geographical considerations with so many counties fringing on London. One of the difficulties is that education has become a political battle-ground since the L.C.C., with its Labour majority, seemed to incline towards replacing the grammar schools in its area by comprehensive schools. The Conservatives, on the other hand, wish to retain the grammar-school system.[1] From the Conservative point of view it may endanger the grammar-school system much more gravely still if a Labour-controlled Greater London Council, responsible for the whole area, were to make a great extension of the comprehensive-school system. The issue closely resembles the nationalisation controversy in that once the conversion is made it is almost impossible to reverse the process.

In general, the Commissions assigned a lower status to the Greater London Boroughs than the Government intends. The Commission's suggestion was for the formation of Boroughs, ranging from 100,000 to 250,000 in population. These Boroughs should be responsible for housing (with some guidance from the Greater London Council), personal health, welfare, child care, environmental health services, apart from refuse disposal which was to be a Council responsibility, and sundry other normal Borough services. To these functions, as has been seen, the Government has added the great responsibility of the education service, but has suggested no other change of function. It has, however, mooted an increase in the size of the Greater London Borough, raising the minimum population from 100,000 to 200,000, presumably with the needs of education chiefly in mind. Amidst all this welter of change the City of London, alone, reinforced by its ancient history, has remained intact. The view of the Commission was that 'Logic has its limits and the position of the City lies outside them',[2] and this the Government supports. The City is to

---

[1] *Report of House of Commons Proceedings*, February 20th, 1962, col. 245. Sir David Eccles, then Minister of Education, referring to the Labour plan, stated 'They know that this plan will not go through so long as there is a Conservative Minister of Education.'

[2] Cmnd. 1164. H.M.S.O. paragraph 935.

receive the additional powers given to Boroughs in the London area.

These changes are most far-reaching. The full effects must still be a matter of speculation. It is reasonable to expect that some services will gain greatly. The organisation of an efficient road system into central London has long been hampered by the parochial nature of the present structure. On this subject the Commission said 'the only possible solution to the present administrative muddle is for the organisation to be firmly in the hands of the Council for Greater London'.[1] The Greater London Council will, therefore, become responsible for the main roads in the area, and will have the help of a strong traffic engineering department. This system could be extended with advantage to the other conurbations in England. From a purely administrative point of view the weakness of the scheme lies in giving too many functions to the new London Boroughs. This is understandable in education, but less so in the assignment of health services to the Boroughs. The local medical committee of the County of London has drawn attention to the fact that it will be neither efficient nor economical to organise on a Borough basis services such as the provision of nurses, midwives, health visitors, and welfare homes for the aged. The bolstering-up of the importance of the London Boroughs will not necessarily result in more democratic management at all, especially if they are given functions which they are not fitted to perform. A breakdown, or the threat of one, in any of the services is likely to lead to the Government superseding the local authorities, which is exactly the situation the Royal Commission was trying to avoid. A planning authority, such as the Greater London Council, democratically elected, and managing the main services with expert help from its local government officials, would give little justification for intervention by the central Government.

The attention of the Commissions has so far, except in Wales, been taken up mainly with the urgent problem of the conurbations. A more logical organisation of the county system in England generally is also probable, reflecting the trend towards amalgamation already in evidence in the report of the Commission on Wales. Wholesale union of counties, except where it is urgent, would be a mistake since it takes time for local opinion to become adapted to changes. Some adjustment of boundaries to compensate for a large

[1] Cmnd. 1164. H.M.S.O. paragraph 779.

town, like Luton in Bedfordshire, being given County Borough status would be feasible. On a larger scale, the amalgamation of counties with largely common interests, such as Cambridge with Huntingdonshire, the Isle of Ely, and the Soke of Peterborough, and Rutland with Leicestershire, are changes which after the initial pangs could be usefully effected. The model towards which the County system needs to work is that put forward by the Local Government Boundary Commission in its investigations of 1946–7. In its Report the Commission suggested that the present counties should be remodelled until their populations reached 200,000 to 1 million. This would not need tremendous changes since many of them are within these limits already. The main point is to ensure that amalgamations do not take place mechanically, but only where there is likely to be an identity of interest among the component parts. The Commission also suggested that 'new County Boroughs' with a population of 60,000–200,000 should be set up to be independent for education, health, and welfare services, but for other main services to be part of the county. This would lessen the present-day objections of County Councils to the grant of County Borough status to thriving towns which henceforward become completely independent. The minimum limit of 60,000, though, seems far too small for efficient administration of health and education services. The retention of the present minimum population of 100,000 for County Borough status is essential. The main hope for towns aiming to achieve County Borough status lies in the amalgamation of counties to make them financially viable without the support of the large towns, which would thus be free to achieve County Borough status. The solution to most of the current problems, therefore, lies in the creation of larger units. Normally, progress in this direction needs to be gradual; historic rights can often be respected; it makes little difference to administration whether the Cinque Port towns, for instance, retain their ancient titles to be Boroughs. Nevertheless, respect for the past ought not to be carried to such an extreme that it conflicts with the needs of the present. This is a situation which is bound to arise when the full scope of the proposed changes becomes apparent.

Another recent development is the revival of the block grant system by the Local Government Act of 1958. In conjunction with the structural changes likely to take place the grant could be of the utmost value in strengthening local authorities. From April, 1959, the County and County Borough Councils have been receiving a general grant, referred to as a block grant, for education (except school meals and milk), agricultural education, health, fire services, and child care. Housing, roads, and police have been excluded from this system, but even so the general grant caters for some highly important services. The assessment of money to be allocated to each service is a matter for the councils, but the Ministers lay down minimum standards to prevent unbalanced use of funds, obviously a necessary proviso. The calculation of the amount of the general grant is based on a formula which takes into account the level of prices, costs, and pay, development plans, probable fluctuation in needs, and population figures, with special reference to the numbers of aged people and of schoolchildren in the area, since their dependence on the social services is greater than for the rest. The grant is made for two- or three-year periods (the first one was for the period April, 1959–April, 1961) thus making it possible to plan ahead. The other sources of revenue — rates, trading services, and loans — are not affected by this change in the grant system; rate deficiency grants will continue to be paid by the Government to poor areas. Rate revenue has been slightly supplemented by the doubling of rates on industrial premises in 1959 from the 25% which they had paid since 1929 to 50%. When the new rating valuation has been completed it is likely that industry will pay the full rate, and so will shops and offices, at present assessed at 80% of the full amount. Revaluation will also affect the householder, involving him in higher rate payments. Even if the general grant is a little less than the local authority would like, therefore, and there is no indication so far of Government parsimony over grants, the small increase in rate-revenue from industry, shops, and householders should help to bridge the difference.

Financially, the scheme is a great improvement on the former system of specific percentage grants, which was both extravagant and unfair. The percentage system did not apply to all services. Where it did apply it was an incentive to high spending in the knowledge that the Government would meet a high proportion, possibly 50%, of the expenditure. The most lavish aid was, therefore, given to areas which could afford to spend most, not to those areas whose need was greatest. It worked unfairly, also, in that services which did not receive a percentage grant were given less attention and revenue than they deserved. Under the new system the councils will be able to develop the services most in need of help. Critics of the scheme accept the wastefulness of the old system, but are dubious about the ability of the councils to administer the various services efficiently, especially education. Criticism was most vociferous when the scheme was instituted, though the critics were basing their attacks largely on hypothesis. The main fear was that, as education was the most expensive service, and as the councillors were supposedly less zealous for educational progress than their critics, education would become a starveling service. Impeccably logical conclusions were then derived from this deduction which would only be convincing if the deduction were fair. This has by no means been established although block grants have been in operation for some time. The critics have been much less in evidence, in fact, since the scheme has been in operation than they were before it started. A suggested alternative is that education and health should be taken out of local hands entirely and administered at national level. This would virtually reduce the County authorities to the level of Borough councils. At the local level, larger authorities strengthen local government, as has been shown, but to imagine that it is logical to remove major services from the large local authorities to give them to the largest authority of all, the central Government, is wildly wrong; this would simply destroy local government.

The outstanding point in favour of the block grant system is that it strengthens the local authorities. In future it looks as if local government will be managed by large authorities with considerable latitude over their financial arrangements. Responsibilities will be greater, and there will be stronger incentives for efficient management and sensible economy. Councillors are likely to be much more aware of their usefulness to the community they serve. The total effect should be a great strengthening of local government in relation to the central Government; if this proves to be so in fact, the recent proposals will mark a change of the greatest significance and value for every citizen. Some sacrifices of local sentiment may be needed, but only on the basis of 'reculer pour mieux sauter'.

FURTHER READING

J. H. Warren, *Municipal Administration* (Pitman, 2nd Edition, 1954).

L. Golding, *Local Government* (English Universities Press, 1959).

W. E. Jackson, *Local Government in England & Wales* (Pelican Books, 1959).

Sir J. Maud and S. E. Finer, *Local Government in England and Wales* (H.U.L., 2nd Edition, 1953).

M. Cole, *Servant of the County* (Dobson, 1956).

II

The Commonwealth
The Problem of Independence

Attitudes to the Commonwealth and Empire. Factors in granting independence: political maturity, social development, industrial organisation, multi-racial problems, economic stability, the problem of the small dependencies. Federation — its limitations and value.

THEME: The methods of training dependencies for self-government are soundly conceived, but cannot be fully applied. This increases the need for a flexible approach.

A balanced assessment of Britain's relationship with the Commonwealth and colonial territories is peculiarly difficult. Present issues are apt to be clouded over with a haze of emotion. There are some who feel a sense of guilt over the way in which the Empire was acquired. They dislike the acquisitive instinct so evident in its formation, the jingoism of painting the world map red, the commercial exploitation of the colonies in the eighteenth and nineteenth centuries, the bitter fighting in India, North America, South Africa, and the Gold Coast, and the over-riding of native interests experienced by the Maoris, for instance, in New Zealand; above all they dislike the bland assumption of a divine right to rule by small groups of white settlers over vastly greater numbers of native inhabitants; nor are they reconciled to the situation by the attempts in the nineteenth and twentieth centuries to create governments on the Westminster model in the dependent territories. Conditioning dependent communities to accept a form of government alien to their own traditions is regarded by these critics as simply another example of British arrogance.

Others, however, regard British policy as simply one of paternalism. Just as a father prepares his son in the manly virtues and then launches him in adult freedom on the world so, too, Britain coaches dependent territories in the arts of democracy, and grants full self-government when the ideal moment has been reached. The newly-fledged Commonwealth country is then free in all aspects of government but, influenced by this benevolent treatment, will, it is hoped, mix a proportion of filial respect with its new equality of status, and co-operate on the whole with British policy out of gratitude. Admittedly, there may have been incidents in the past which native populations find it hard to forget. But these are wiped out by the dedicated services of British administrators, mission-aries, and social workers, labouring together to train the dependent territories to accept one of the best forms of government in the world.

Both these views contain elements of truth, but both are far too simple to be accurate. For those who are hag-ridden by guilt and who have no faith in the right of the British to train native popula-tions in our own habits of government the only justifiable policy now is to cut the links abruptly, leaving the native territories to work out their own salvation with some assistance from the United Nations. This suggestion was more popular before the recent events in the Belgian Congo, where the consequences of a sudden withdrawal of a colonising power have been clearly demonstrated. British withdrawals from colonies have been less abrupt, but the disorders following the grant of independence to India and Paki-stan in 1947 give an indication within our own experience of the dangers of leaving territories to manage themselves when there is a risk of internal conflict. Empires, as Thucydides knew over two thousand years ago, are even harder to lay down than they are to acquire. To jettison an Empire creates more problems than it solves.

The idea of paternalism has more to commend it as it is an attempt at a constructive policy to deal with present problems. Yet the 'paternal' analogy is a very imperfect one. It is obvious when a son attains his twenty-first birthday, but not at all obvious when a state becomes adult. The son comes of the same stock as his father; his circumstances and habits of thought are intrinsically very similar, but there are vast differences in these respects between Britain and the dependent territories. Moreover, it would be a singularly unfortunate father whose son's emergence to adulthood was preceded by the agitation and violence which are commonplace in Commonwealth history. Canada in the nineteenth century, South Africa, India, Eire, Ghana, and Cyprus in the twentieth century, all achieved self-government soon after periods of violence, and there is little doubt that the violence accelerated the process.

Paternalism, therefore, is a loose description of the relationship, but there is a policy consciously applied towards the colonies which is strongly influenced by the desire to make the transition to self-government as painless as possible. The policy is constantly being adapted. Pressure of opinion at the United Nations, from our friends as well as our opponents, pressure from sections of the British Press, and above all, explosive agitation for independence within the colonies, influence the pace of the movement towards self-government. To choose the ideal moment for the grant of independence is not always possible, therefore, but there is a general pattern visible in the features of British colonial policy, especially since 1945.

Ideally, certain requirements need to be fulfilled before a colony attains independence. The object of the Colonial Office is to prepare the dependent territories as fully as possible for self-government, though this work often cannot be carried through to its completion, because of the various pressures mentioned. One of the first requirements is that the colony should be politically mature, by which we mean that it is ready to adopt a democratic form of government. Although dependent territories are free to establish whatever form of government they choose on attaining independence, their training under British administration is in democratic procedures with the hope that they will adopt a government of this type. All the Commonwealth countries, except Pakistan, are in form democracies,[1] based either on the Westminster model, or on the American system with a President as Head of State. Democracies cannot work effectively unless there is an electorate sufficiently well-informed and critical to be able to make an intelligent choice between the contending parties. Any colony on the verge of independence should be able to provide all its citizens with a basic education. In practice, this ideal cannot be fully attained in the time available. In Britain itself the standard of general education lagged far behind political development for centuries; it was not until 1891 that it could be said that there was a free, national, com-

[1] In Tanganyika, Ghana, Kenya, and Malawi the one-party system seems likely to prevail now (September 1964).

pulsory system of elementary education, although the vote had been widely extended by the Acts of 1867 and 1884.

The gap between political development and the educational development which gives substance to the forms of democracy is equally apparent in the newly independent Commonwealth territories. Nor is this surprising. The size of the Commonwealth countries — Nigeria, for instance, is nearly four times the size of Britain — the dispersion of their populations, the sheer physical difficulty of getting to schools, and the rapidity of the movement towards self-government have all contrived to make it peculiarly difficult to organise a satisfactory system of primary education. These problems are particularly relevant in India, Pakistan, and the African territories.[1] Ghana, the first of the native African states to gain Commonwealth status and the prospective leader of the pan-African movement, provides a good example. Its secondary and higher education is of fairly recent origin, but it is of good quality; on the other hand, it was not until after independence was given that a comprehensive attempt was made to build primary schools in sufficient numbers for the country's needs. The top-heaviness of the system helps to explain some of the recent incidents in Ghana which have caused so much disquiet. The rulers have been educated to a high standard, often reinforced by a period of further education in Britain. The masses, who have moved at bewildering speed from the primitive context of tribal life to the complexities of modern civilisation, have lacked the education to adapt them to the change. Measures taken by Dr. Nkrumah may have seemed distasteful by our standards, but circumstances are very different there, as he has been at pains to point out. Moreover, if so basic a service as primary education is inadequate, the responsibility is in some measure our own. The critics of the present regime are sometimes those who were most insistent that our continued presence in the Gold Coast was wrong; yet, ideally, a longer period of British rule might have been justified to ensure a balanced development of the social services before independence was given. An essential preliminary should be a complete framework of primary and secondary schools together with university colleges for higher education. The education sections of the Colonial Office and of the United Nations have worked towards this

[1] See *Parliamentary Affairs*, Spring 1964, pp. 160–71, for an instructive article by John Day on the problems of democracy in Africa.

objective, but the pace of events, politically, has left them stranded.

Political education of the African administrations has proceeded more successfully. British officials have stayed on after independence, as they did in Ghana, but their role is an entirely subordinate one. African leaders, such as Nkrumah in Ghana and Balewa in Nigeria, do not need to be propped up by Civil Servants. This is partly due to their own gifts, but partly also to the political training which has been one of the best features of the British Colonial system. Early political development in colonies destined for independence follows a set pattern. Nomination by the Governor of a few native members to join the British representatives in the Legislative Council, the embryo Parliament, is the first step. By gradual stages, usually based at first on property qualifications, a full electoral system is introduced. The British officials in the Legislative Council are reduced in numbers until the Legislative Council consists entirely of native elected members. Meanwhile, a similar process is at work in the Executive Council, which is the embryo Cabinet. The Governor, by selection from the Legislative Council, includes a few native members in the Executive Council which previously would have consisted entirely of British officials. Eventually, native members are given charge of some Government departments until, finally, a full Ministerial system is introduced on the British model. The Governor's powers then gradually recede until his functions are the same as those of the Queen in Britain. By that time the Colony is ready for independence. The process may often be less gradual than would be ideal, but it gives enough time for the leaders to study the techniques of law-making, debate and administration. Political leaders, like Balewa, Nkrumah, Nyerere in Tanganyika, and Tengku Abdul Rahman in Malaysia, have been facing problems, which, in their different context, are quite as testing as those which face the statesmen of western Europe; without a sound political training they would be quite unable to do so. Administrative mistakes are made of a kind which one would not expect in Britain. Matters involving expertise of a specialist kind such as clear wording of parliamentary bills are sometimes not very well managed. But it is more to the point that the administrative system works so remarkably well, considering the brief duration of independence of the post-war Commonwealth countries.

In local administration Africans are well fitted to manage their own affairs. Local government under the tribal system had been firmly established in Africa for centuries when the British arrived. The wise guidance of Lord Lugard, who by the doctrine of Indirect Rule adapted the existing system of local government in Nigeria to fit in with the central administration, created a model relationship which has been imitated in East and Central Africa and in the newer territories of the Commonwealth. Since independence occasional changes have been made affecting local government structure. Ghana, for instance, has been divided into six regions, each under an African politician, but no radical regroupings have been necessary. This is natural enough since the existing units of local government follow racial, territorial, and religious boundaries, so that local government does not present any great specific difficulties. It is a natural growth of long duration; central Government, on the other hand, is a forced plant and correspondingly fragile.

The physical needs, relating to health problems and working conditions, require as much forethought as matters of education and political training. One way of gaining increased awareness of the social problems of the newer Commonwealth territories is to visualise the somewhat similar problems which faced British politicians in the nineteenth century. During the course of that century there were many social reforms affecting public health, local government, industry, and the trade unions. These reforms provided protection for the citizen against bad management. Similar problems face the colonial administrators. Medical aid and training are given through the World Health Organisation of the United Nations, and through the Medical Section of the Colonial Office. These organisations are not large enough to meet all the needs of the situation — no existing organisation could be — as the outbreak of serious diseases in India and Pakistan has shown. Although great progress has been made from the time when West Africa, for instance, was known as 'the white man's grave' the level of training in matters of health and hygiene is still appreciably lower than in Britain; admittedly, climatic conditions accentuate the difficulties. The fact that health problems have little bearing on politics is an advantage, however, since it makes little difference whether the doctors are European or African so long as the diseases are cured. Trained medical experts can stay on in ex-colonies much longer than European administrators without their presence there providing an affront to national pride.

Trade Union organisations able to secure fair hours, reasonable wages, and good working conditions, also need to be firmly established before independence is given. Since industrialisation is a comparatively new phenomenon in the post-war Commonwealth countries it might be expected that the principles of Trade Unionism would not be readily understood. If that were true it would militate against the grant of independence since the future welfare of the mass of the workers is an important consideration. In fact these countries have adapted themselves with surprising speed to the ideas of Trade Unionism. This may be caused, in part, by the fact that the idea of concerted action, as a protection against any abuse of workers' interests by the employers, has something in common with the mass sentiment of nationalism often directed against political authority as a preliminary to independence. Apart from fitting in with current moods and attitudes Trade Unionism has also gained strength from the specific guidance which has been given by the Colonial Office and by the Trades Union Congress. In areas where there is extreme poverty, as in parts of India and in some of the West Indian islands, the objectives for which the Unions strive are naturally limited by the acute hardship of living conditions there; Trade Unions by their nature work far better where there is wealth inequitably distributed than where there is no wealth at all. Africa has its slums and poverty too, but with its great natural resources provides a situation favourable to the rapid growth of Trade Unionism. Trade Unions there have in fact made rapid advances towards federation, a more sophisticated level of development than is involved in the existence merely of Unions for the separate industries. There is strong support for the All-African Trade Union Conference, though Mr. Mboya, the influential African nationalist from Kenya, clings to support for the Socialist International Confederation of Free Trade Unions. The aims of Unionism are broadly the same as in Britain. Where differences occur they are in method as in Ghana, where Union membership is compulsory, an instance of the more authoritarian approach visible in the newer Commonwealth countries.

Whether suitable political and social organisation has been developed or not, additional factors can influence the pace of the movement towards independence. Multi-racial communities, in particular, have problems which may seem incapable of solution without the serious risk of oppression of minorities. The racial factor has not greatly hampered the movement towards independence of Ghana and Nigeria in West Africa, but in East and Central Africa, and in Cyprus, racial considerations are of the utmost importance and they have a strong bearing, too, on the policies of the Malaysian Federation. In Kenya the problem is partly how to reconcile the interests of a small minority of educated Europeans, accustomed to political and economic dominance, with the interests of a large African population, often illiterate, but inspired by their native leaders to press for independence. But there is also the complication involved in the presence of other races, such as Indians and Arabs. In the Central African Federation the grouping of the two Rhodesias and of Nyasaland has illustrated that unions of this kind cannot be solidly based merely on geographic and economic convenience. Racial separatism is too strong an emotion to be outweighed by material advantage, as Dr. Banda's determined opposition to federation has shown, for Nyasaland (Malawi) seems scarcely viable economically as a separate state. The basic antipathy of black men towards white rule, and of white men towards black rule cannot be overcome by the belief that it has been outgrown; in the shifting pattern of political structures in Africa there is hope of solution, as will be seen later, but not by making assumptions that racial antagonisms are purely superficial. In some areas the situation is less flexible than in Africa, so that the only possibility is to work out a *modus vivendi* on the existing basis. Racial differences in Cyprus between Greeks and Turks, and in Malaysia between Malayans and Chinese cannot be obviated by territorial regroupings.

In these multi-racial communities it will require an imaginative and adaptable approach to achieve any solution to the problem of government. The hope of a friendly constructive agreement has often been destroyed before the delegates sit at the conference table by the bitterness of the struggles which have gone before. Archbishop Makarios, Jomo Kenyatta, and Dr. Hastings Banda have all had experience of prison or exile because of their association with militant nationalism. Yet, paradoxically, the violent nationalist desire for independence can be an obstacle to it. There is a natural wish to ensure that minorities will not be victimised upon the withdrawal of British rule, but this is difficult to guarantee where long-standing hatreds have eaten away respect for individual freedoms; violence directed against British rule could swiftly be turned upon other alien minority groups. The outbreak of violence in India and Pakistan, when they were given their independence in 1947, led to many deaths of Hindus in Pakistan, and of Moslems in India. It would be culpably irresponsible to grant independence to a country if it led to a repetition of these 1947 events. Yet time is short, nationalism is explosive, and it is wildly optimistic to hope that in a few years it can be possible to inculcate native populations in dependent territories with the traditional restraints shown in Britain towards minority groups. Clearly, the multi-racial communities are posing problems which are difficult even to comprehend in Britain, and which are certainly likely to prevent a perfect solution, or even a very satisfactory one, in some parts of the Commonwealth and Empire. In this connection it is important to realise that the existing frontiers in Africa are largely the result of European imperialism in the nineteenth century. Once the controlling hand of the European is removed the old tribal frontiers will acquire a new relevance and old hostilities are likely to revive. This has been seen already in Uganda, Kenya, and Nigeria. The conventional war for adjustment of frontiers, which appears to be outmoded in modern Europe, may take on a new lease of life in Africa unless the new states there show a more international outlook than has been common in Europe.

A further factor to consider in granting independence is the economic stability of the dependency. Where there are good natural resources, as there are in Ghana and Nigeria, independence involves little risk of hardship. Ghana in particular has launched an ambitious development scheme involving improvements in communications, the £200 million Volta River project — made possible by exploitation of the well-established trade in cocoa — research into newer sources of wealth such as oil and minerals, and the erection of many modern buildings. Enough confidence has been created to attract foreign capital from America and from West Germany among other countries.[1] Most of the African territories have enough natural resources to provide reasonable security for the future, except Nyasaland and small somewhat isolated territories like Sierra Leone. Yet in India poverty is tragically rife, and in another quarter of the world, the West Indies, the break-down

[1] See the article 'Royalty and Revolutionaries' by Colin Legum in the *Observer* of November 22nd, 1959, on this point, and also for a more detailed assessment of political and economic development in Ghana.

of the Caribbean Federation means that the Windward and Lee-
ward groups of islands, remote and deficient in resources, must
remain dependent on British help. An undue dependence on outside aid is a great source of weakness since it can make political
independence an empty form. The subsidies which Britain provides through the Colonial Development Corporation gradually
cease to flow when independence has been attained. In 1958 the
Government made it plain that after independence projects
already started would continue to be helped through the Corporation but not new ones. Help may come through the World Bank,
but in general the new Commonwealth territories cannot launch
out on the new developments they would like unless foreign
investors can be filled with enough confidence to risk their capital
in the hope of a good return. The chances of their doing so can be
estimated with reasonable accuracy by the Colonial Office before
self-government is granted; this factor of economic stability is yet
another consideration in the grant of independence. The main
interest of investors is profit, and they cannot be expected to make
contributions out of altruism.

The factors which have been studied so far relate primarily to the
large dependencies with sufficient resources in population and
wealth to be self-sufficient ultimately if not immediately. There
still remain a large number of scattered small dependencies, some
placed in a special category because of their strategic importance,
like Malta, Gibraltar, and Singapore, and others, relics of our
history, which are very tiny, like Pitcairn Island with its 130 inhabitants, Mauritius, and the Seychelles Islands. The strategic
reasons which once made Malta and Singapore of such great
significance have lost some of their importance through changing
methods of warfare. The American emphasis on powerfully armed,
thoroughly organised task forces, such as their Seventh Fleet, and
on an underwater fleet depending for its needs simply on a mother
ship, has led recently to some re-assessment of the need for the
retention of British bases overseas. They are expensive to maintain
and it may be that some of them are outmoded. Each needs to be
judged on its own merits. Singapore is very vulnerable; it is possibly
less vital now as a base in view of the firm establishment of American
forces in the Far East. Since it has been integrated with the Federation of Malaysia use of the base will become subject to Malaysian
approval, diminishing the certainty of its effectiveness still further.

These considerations apply to some extent to Malta and Gibraltar. Malta was used as a base during the attack on Egypt, and for the limited operations which may arise in the Middle East it might continue to be useful. Retention of a base there, however, ought not to rest merely on habitual thinking where preparations are made to meet situations which no longer exist. Egyptian control of the Suez Canal and the diminished influence of Britain in Arabian countries have detracted from the value of Mediterranean bases. The fluidity of politics in the Middle East is probably the best reason for maintaining the *status quo* in Malta and in Gibraltar; it may be that their significance will revive, even though at the moment the practical value strategically of Malta in particular seems very slight. Complete political freedom for these strategically placed dependencies is not yet likely simply on the grounds of their potential military importance.[1] Since Malta has close ties with Britain, springing from her part in the last war and the number of Maltese who have come to Britain, it has been suggested that the best political solution would be integration with Britain. Presumably this would place Malta in the same constitutional position as Northern Ireland. She would send two or three members to Westminster to participate in debates there. The scheme does not sound very convincing. The closeness of Northern Ireland to Britain, and economic and social similarities give its union with Britain some reality. British and Maltese interests do not overlap sufficiently to make it worthwhile for Malta to have separate representation at Westminster.

Even if integration should prove to be the best solution for Malta's future there remain many small territories for whom neither integration nor federation is feasible. The Labour Party's proposal in 1957 was that these small territories should be given Dominion status and they would presumably have complete control over internal and external affairs, including the right to withhold the use of bases from Britain. The aim of the proposal was to give these small areas the same right as independent nations to manage their own affairs and to take on commitments of their own choosing. One weakness in the scheme is that the complete freedom envisaged can hardly be possible where economic aid continues to be required. There is abundant evidence in recent history of the

---

[1] Malta's independence (September, 1964) leaves Britain's military rights there intact.

way in which economic aid has been the prelude to political infil-
tration. It is also extremely debatable whether a small dependency
would have leaders sufficiently knowledgeable to chart a course
through the intricacies of foreign relations. This is particularly so
if it had value as a military base as a result of which it could easily
become the victim of the ingenious pressures which larger states
can bring to bear. In internal affairs, on the other hand, there is no
reason why these small powers should not be able to manage the
great bulk of their own affairs through Legislative and Executive
Councils. Admittedly this approach means that the small dependencies will never be able to attain complete self-government, but a
passion for exact equality of status amongst all Commonwealth
countries from Canada to Pitcairn Island appears to be misguided
in placing a greater burden on the smaller dependencies than they
are able to carry. If in addition they became the objectives for the
great powers manoeuvring for positions of advantage the dangers
involved for them would be much greater than anything they are
experiencing at the moment.

The problem of the small dependencies shows how necessary it
is to maintain some flexibility of approach towards these greatly
varying territories. To visualise the movement towards independence as a process in mass production is unrealistic. Another
instance of the need for broad vision lies in the recent suggestions
for federation. Difficulties in the Caribbean Federation and in the
Central African Federation have brought the federal idea into disrepute. Yet in each of these areas the break-down has been produced by specific local factors, economic in the Caribbean Federation and racial in Central Africa, which need not apply elsewhere.
Canada and Australia provide examples of territories where
federation in its present-day form has not produced disorder and
discontent. To make federation work there must be a real community of interest, especially racially; the geographical unity of the
area needs to be sufficiently a reality to make communication
reasonably easy, unlike the islands of the West Indies scattered
over a thousand miles of sea; above all, post-war history has shown
that federation has little chance of success if it is imposed against
the wishes of large numbers of the inhabitants. Economic advantage
is not sufficiently powerful a factor to compensate for the slights
on nationalist feeling which an imposed solution continually
produces.

Bearing these factors in mind it may well be that two recent imaginative proposals for federation have much to commend them. The first one, put forward by Dr. Nyerere from Tanganyika, has the initial advantage of emanating from an African rather than a European leader in a continent where the former are so preponderant. His suggestion is that the East African territories of Uganda, Kenya, Tanganyika, and Zanzibar, the first three already having some experience of working together under the East African High Commission, should federate with Northern Rhodesia and Nyasaland, thus detaching two territories where African nationalist feeling is strong from the Central African Federation.[1] Possibly the Federation could become larger still with the addition of the High Commission territory of Bechuanaland which shares a common frontier with Northern Rhodesia.[2] Encouragement of the scheme would be a positive way of showing sympathy towards African nationalism, nor are the difficulties insurmountable. The territories are adjacent to each other and, although communications between Central and East Africa would need to be improved, that problem in modern times is not so intractable as it once was. Economically, Northern Rhodesia, Tanganyika, and Kenya have sufficient natural resources to make the Federation prosper. Political problems would present difficulties, particularly the allocation of power to the Central Federal government. Problems of this kind are greatly eased by good-will, however, and if at first anyway the Federal government were a guiding and advisory body, especially on matters of common interest involving economic affairs and communications, the scheme should have a good chance of working well. A second political problem is that the creation of such a Federation would virtually isolate Southern Rhodesia, which might join the Federation itself, though this is unlikely, or else harness her affairs more closely with the neighbouring territory of South Africa. A further difficulty lies in the internal disagreements in Uganda, though the creation of a larger unit may submerge local discords. Ideal solutions for the complexities of the

[1] The leaders of Kenya, Tanganyika, and Uganda agreed on June 5th, 1963, to establish a federation which they hoped would be the basis of a wider grouping still. Tanganyika and Zanzibar were federated in April, 1964.

[2] The article by C. Legum, 'Doom and Promise' in the *Observer* of November 27th, 1960, contains a stimulating analysis of the Nyerere scheme.

African situation are likely to be endlessly evasive, but the Nyerere scheme shows a breadth of vision and, at the same time, a respect for the realities of the African situation which deserve sympathetic appraisal. It is more soundly based in principle than the Central African Federation and more worthy of trial.

The second scheme under consideration within the Commonwealth is for an extension of the Malayan Federation to bring in Singapore and the dependencies of North Borneo (Sabah), and Sarawak.[1] The scheme has several weaknesses. One of the mainsprings of the suggestion is Malayan concern over Singapore, partly because Commonwealth use of it as a base might involve Malaya itself in the repercussions of conflict, partly because the large number of Chinese in Singapore might be a threat to Malaya if Singapore gained independence separately. The situation is made more complex by the fact that Singapore is still a base for the Commonwealth powers in fulfilling their obligations to the South East Asia Treaty Organisation; this may remain so in spite of the build-up of American strength in this part of the world. These matters of high policy are apt to obscure the fact that in modern times an imposed Federation has little chance of success, and that ultimately the most cogent factor of all is the willingness of inhabitants to accept a federal scheme. The crucial point is the attitude of the people themselves in Singapore. A further difficulty in the suggestion lies in the scattered nature of the proposed federation. Sarawak at its nearest point is some 400 miles from Malaya and North Borneo 900 miles. Federation has some superficial attractions in that it groups together with an appearance of neatness territories which would otherwise be isolated, but in relation to the other issues involved this is a secondary consideration. Each scheme has to be considered on its own merits. In Africa circumstances favour the idea of federation if it is based on African nationalism; the Malaysian scheme, on the other hand, has much less to commend it, except expediency.

The Empire was acquired by accident and there is some danger that it may be lost in the same way. There is, undoubtedly, an underlying purpose in Colonial Office policy; its aim of training the dependencies in the arts of self-government is wholly laudable. Yet it would be complacent to believe that this purpose can be fulfilled to a degree which is even satisfactory. Political and nationalist

[1] This federation has now been set up (September 16th, 1963).

pressure, and the constant jockeying for strategic advantage between the Western powers and their possible enemies make it impossible for an exact design and timetable to be observed. The greatest danger is a dull uniformity of approach which ignores the complex and differing interplay of circumstances affecting the various dependencies. A recognition, based on something more than lip service, that the old relationship between European and native inhabitants can no longer be maintained, and a flexibility of approach towards ideas for federation, integration, or even continuing dependence, offer the best hope of a Commonwealth and Empire with a true sense of unity.

FURTHER READING

J. Coatman, *The British Family of Nations* (Harrap, 1950).

Sir Ivor Jennings, *The Approach to Self Government* (C.U.P., 1956).

M. Wight, *The Development of the Legislative Council 1606–1945* (Faber, 1947).

Sir C. Jeffries, *The Colonial Office* (Allen & Unwin, 1956).

D. Austin, *West Africa and the Commonwealth* (Pelican Books, 1957).

J. Strachey, *The End of Empire* (Gollancz, 1959).

K. C. Wheare, *The Constitutional Structure of the Commonwealth* (Oxford — Clarendon Press, 1960).

12

The Strengths and Weaknesses of the British Constitution

Changing conditions are leading to stronger Executive control. Formal restraints on the Executive are negligible. The only counter-balance is public opinion. The degree of freedom of the Judiciary, of local government, and of the citizen, in relation to central Government.

THEME: Greater central control is largely involuntary in Britain, but the freedoms are losing their value and need to be actively championed.

The inability of constitutional commentators to isolate the British constitution, to dissect it, and duly hold up the parts for inspection, is often a source of insular satisfaction. The constitution of Britain is unknowable, like its weather, and the pride taken in both has a similar quality. It may be that there is merit in a constitutional flexibility which makes Governments continuously responsive to the wishes of the people, and it is still possible to take this optimistic view of the working of the British system of government. But flexibility carries with it dangers too. In a constitution resting ultimately on the intangible factor of public opinion the guarantees of individual freedom are extremely fragile. Habits of thought change. The degree of State control which has become commonplace now would have seemed an outrageous intrusion on private rights one hundred years ago, and there is good reason to believe that the strengthening of the Executive in the modern state is a process which has by no means reached its culmination. The speed and ease with which the traditionally slow-moving British democracy can transform itself into an authoritarian state in war-time, without any need to diverge from normal constitutional usage, is a sharp reminder that governmental methods in Britain can easily be akin to those of dictatorship.

In the emergency of war these methods are necessary, for the preservation of the state is the first duty of government. The current problem, however, is that emergency conditions have far outlasted the war itself. The close-knit relationship and rivalry of so many nations of the world in politics, strategy, and finance have produced the now familiar situation in which distant threats, or stock-market fluctuations, produce repercussions throughout great sectors of the world with the utmost speed. Recurrent crises in the post-war era have conditioned Governments into a frame of mind where the possible use of emergency powers is always close to the surface. Peace is a misnomer for the conditions which have applied since 1945, when it would be difficult to point to any time when fighting was not going on in some quarter of the world. This may always have been true in world history, but now the risks are incomparably greater. The destructive power and speed of modern warfare have undoubtedly given some justification for the increase of Executive powers not only in Britain but elsewhere.

Recent tendencies in internal policies have accentuated this movement towards greater Executive control. The precariousness of the economy in Britain since the war has increasingly made it evident that the freedom of Victorian times is entirely inappropriate to efficient management of the country's finance. The uneven way in which the pay-pause policy of the Government has had to be applied shows the essential difficulty in Britain of working towards objectives which are nationally desirable without infringing individual freedom. There is strong reason to believe that this dilemma is much more likely to be solved by a further extension of central control than by a return to nineteenth-century 'laissez-faire'. Attitudes are changing. Some of the freedoms for which our ancestors struggled have lost their reality. Freedom of religion in a country where only a minority take part in regular formal worship has lost much of its old significance. Freedom of speech and of assembly have a diminished value in a political system where Governments, secure behind the barrier a disciplined party can provide between elections, are not notably responsive to public opinion. Freedom of property is no longer sacrosanct since the central Government has used the power of compulsory purchase.

These changes are recognisable features of modern society. The danger involved in the steady erosion of individual freedoms is obvious enough. The point of greater interest is to discover whether there are any assured limitations to the authority of the State over the citizen in Britain. Is there, perhaps, some inner citadel of freedom which is certain to remain intact short of the supreme emergency of war itself?

If formal assurances were sought the prospects would be bleak indeed. So far as we have any written constitution at all it consists of a few historic statutes and in the judge-made law of the courts. It would be entirely legal and constitutional for these slender protections to be swept away altogether by new Acts of Parliament. Since Parliament can be claimed to be representative of the people this great power would seem to matter little. Any great changes in our constitutional habits would, in effect, be sanctioned by the people themselves and would be correspondingly acceptable. Yet much of this traditional view is a polite fiction. The concept of the Sovereignty of Parliament has steadily been drained of significance ever since the wide extensions of the franchise from 1867 onwards. Policy is fashioned and decisions taken not by Parliament, nor by the House of Commons, nor even by the majority party to any great extent, but by the Cabinet and Prime Minister. There is nothing new about this. It was evident during the ministries of Disraeli and of Lord Salisbury and has become increasingly obvious ever since. The situation has been worsened by the existence of a third party, resulting more often than not in the election of a Government supported by less than half the voters. As has been pointed out already (see Chapter 7) the ideal solution for this would be the union of the main anti-conservative parties to form a Radical party, though there seems little hope at the moment that the Labour and Liberal Parties will ever be able to agree on a common programme.

This would only be a partial answer to the problem. The question of the limitations to State action still remains unanswered. The words of historic documents give no permanent assurance of freedom; nor do the words uttered inside and outside Parliament if they are divorced from the power of influencing decisions. Nor is there any longer the balance of power between the main institutions of government which Montesquieu believed to exist when he visited Britain in 1732 to study the constitution. His findings were published in 1748 as *L'Esprit des Lois* and make an interesting comparison with the organisation of power in modern times. He was impressed by the judicious division which made one section of government act as restraint on another. The King and Ministers comprised the Executive. They controlled the armed forces, foreign policy, and with Parliament's consent levied taxation. Parliament was the Legislature, and besides controlling taxation gave annual consent for the continuance in being of the armed forces, and had some limited powers of calling Ministers to account. The Judiciary was virtually independent in its actions, subject to its duty of enforcing the statutory law passed by Parliament. It has been pointed out that Montesquieu's analysis was not completely accurate; there was greater fusion of the powers than he thought. But this is largely a quibble. In the early years of the eighteenth century a balance of power was very nearly achieved. No single branch of government could claim complete dominance. The monarchy had abandoned its claims to absolute supremacy and no institution had arrogated to itself similar powers. Since that time each century has witnessed changes in the constitutional relationship of the divisions of government and each change has brought closer the risk of destroying the balance completely. This is not an argument against change. The governmental system of the eighteenth century was notoriously imperfect and unrepresentative, but it is an argument against floating helplessly with the tide of constitutional change without realising the consequences. In the nineteenth century it was Parliament which extended its powers in the face of a decorous rearguard action by the monarchy persisting into the last years of the century, when it became the strictly limited constitutional monarchy with which all are familiar. Having won that battle Parliament now settled its internal struggle by making the House of Lords subordinate to the House of Commons by the Parliament Act of 1911, reinforced later by that of 1949. Yet, all this time, the Cabinet was extending its hold over the branches of government and over Parliament itself, until now there is no doubt of its dominance.

It might seem, therefore, that the balance of power has been completely destroyed. The extension of the franchise has removed any possibility of the House of Lords acting as a check upon a Government determined to have its own way. The monarchy, though not entirely negligible in influence potentially, could only oppose governmental action in the unlikely event of being assured of mass public support in doing so. The House of Commons for a variety of reasons, some of them unavoidable in the circumstances of modern times, cannot bring to bear on governmental policy the critical scrutiny which ought to be the essential strength of our system. Of the various institutions which at different times have struggled for supreme authority in the State, the Cabinet alone has increased its strength. Firmly guided by the Prime Minister, supported by party loyalty, buttressed by party discipline and the workings of our electoral system, aided by the administrative expertise of the Civil Service, and fed with information by the large numbers of planning and research units, the Cabinet seems to have obtained a position of unassailable power. Act of Parliament is the supreme law, and it is the Cabinet, almost exclusively, which initiates the important Acts of Parliament.

Against this formidable power all that can be set in the scales is the imponderable of public opinion. So far as there is a balance of power in Britain today it is achieved by the force of public opinion. The limits of power are the limits of public tolerance. But these limits change. The public is far more ready now to accept State control than it once was. Yet there are limits, not very clearly discerned perhaps, but still of the utmost value as restraints on the growing power of the Executive. What then are the essential features which still command respect and whose continued survival gives some reasonable guarantee of freedom for the citizen? One of the most important guarantees is undoubtedly the continued independence of judicial proceedings, and on this there is fortunately still a high degree of sensitivity in Britain. The great bulk of judicial work is divorced from political considerations, but the interest roused by the semi-political offences committed in the demonstrations for nuclear disarmament has shown a keen public awareness over the crucial issues. The degree of force permissible to the police in dealing with passive disobedience, the rights of the accused in court, and the nature of the punishment imposed have all rightly received considerable publicity. Another recent matter in which public interest has been shown concerns the working of the administrative tribunals. It was a healthy sign that sufficient disquiet arose over the use of these tribunals by Government Departments to lead to the setting-up of the Franks Committee and to subsequent Government action in the Administrative Tribunals Act of 1958. Public opinion and governmental action do not always coincide in this way, but it is reassuring that both Governments and governed accept the impartiality of judicial proceedings as vital.

Local government is another sphere in which at least a degree of independence of central Government is crucial in a state with respect for freedom. Full independence is scarcely possible. The need to maintain a reasonable uniformity of standard, coupled with the fact that over half of local government revenue comes from Government grants, means that much of local government policy is controlled from the centre. This control is generally unobtrusive and local government, reinforced by the 1958 Act, by its electoral system, and by its use of unpaid councillors, shows a reasonable degree of independence. Party politics are firmly established in local government, but councillors, with their greater independence of status, are not so party-conscious as members of the House of Commons. The balance between central control and local independence is fairly maintained, and any undesirable extension of governmental influence over local affairs would be very conspicuous to the many thousands of councillors and to Opposition M.P.s. This is a good guarantee for the continuance of the limited freedom existing in local government at the moment.

Judicial and local government activities are specialised aspects of government. Important though they are, it is Government policy and legislation, with their direct impact on the citizen, which command more attention. There are restraints which Parliament can bring to bear upon governmental actions but only in extreme circumstances. Public opinion can often find more effective expression through group action than it can through the House of Commons; it is expression of public opinion in this way rather than through political representation which now constitutes the strongest barrier against unpopular Government action. It should be pointed out in fairness that this notion of barriers, and of a division between Government and people is sometimes said to be a false one; that Government and people are one. But this identification is absurd in a country where the electoral system seldom produces a majority Government, and where the intricacies of governing make it impossible for the public to play any real part in determining policy. Government is by the expert rather than by the people, not through any malicious design, but through the complexities of modern life. It might be considered for instance

that Britain's entry into the Common Market should have been
made the subject of a referendum, since this step might lead to a
constitutional change. But a 'yes' or 'no' answer to a question of
such difficulty would have such varying value, according to the
extent of information of the voter, that it could not be a sound
basis for a policy decision. There are many matters, in foreign and
economic policy especially, where all the voter can do is to leave
the decision to the politicians whom he has put in power. He will
rarely be able to express worthwhile approval or disapproval of
decisions which have been made, simply because the ramifications
of policy are now so extensive that only an expert with all the
information at his disposal can accurately assess the merits of
foreign policy and economic measures.

This also applies, though with somewhat less force, to many
matters of domestic policy. There are limits, however, which no
Government has the right to infringe, and which ought to be plain
to any citizen with a knowledge of the basic freedoms. Freedom of
speech, of association, of assembly, and governmental respect for
the judicial system, are fundamental rights still potentially of the
greatest importance in any free society. Each of these freedoms is
basically concerned with the right to express dissent without fear
of retribution by the State; this must be backed, too, by the willingness of the State to right a legitimate grievance if the freedoms are
to have any real significance. The danger in modern society is that,
while there is freedom to express dissent, the means of securing a
remedy for grievances may well deter all but the most persistent. It
is that which has led to the suggestion that Britain should have an
Ombudsman, a 'grievance man' as there is in Denmark, sufficiently
influential to make his opinions respected by Government
Departments. This suggestion, as has been previously indicated
(Chapter 5), is unlikely to be fulfilled in Britain, but a House of
Commons Committee, or a Parliamentary Commissioner performing similar functions is feasible. Criticism of the present procedure
in the House of Commons for safeguarding citizens' interests is
implicit in these suggestions and this is naturally a matter for concern. It is hopeful, however, that there is sufficient sensitivity to
the rights of individual citizens for these suggestions to be put
forward and to be given serious consideration by the Government.
The Treasury Solicitor, Sir Harold Kent, has stated that the idea
of an Ombudsman on the Danish model would conflict with the

British idea of Ministerial Responsibility.[1] This need not apply if there were a House of Commons Committee.

In spite of the now familiar background of emergencies, which itself justifies a greater degree of State control than was once necessary, the essential freedoms in Britain appear to have survived. They are not so firmly established as they were, but are still sufficiently vigorous to give reality to the description of our society as a 'free' one. It should be clear, however, that these freedoms cannot retain their full significance unless they are actively maintained. It is not sufficient to believe that tradition alone is the only safeguard required for the citizen's rights. A study of the changing attitudes towards the freedoms since Stuart times would show how unwise it is to pin overmuch hope on precedent in the direct relationship between Government and citizen. The best protection of all comes not from the past, but from the present, in the existence of vigilant, well-informed public opinion.

[1] At a United Nations seminar on judicial remedies against administrative abuses of power, 1962. See also pp. 73–74.

FURTHER READING

Sir Ivor Jennings, *The British Constitution* (C.U.P., 1958).
J. P. Mackintosh, *The British Cabinet* (Stevens, 1962).

Comments on Further Reading

SOME readers, particularly in schools, may be grateful for advice on textbooks where concise statements on the factual background of the institutions described may be found. Two short books of value in this respect are *Government in Great Britain, the Empire, and the Commonwealth* (Cambridge University Press, 3rd Edition, 1963) by L. W. White and W. D. Hussey, and *Whitehall — Town Hall* (George Harrap and Co. Ltd., 1960) by F. W. G. Benemy. *The British Constitution* (Macmillan and Co. Ltd., 1963) by J. Harvey and L. Bather is a very painstaking and useful analysis of their subject.

There are several books which range widely over the different aspects of the working of the British constitution, and which serve as a good preparation for the detailed study of special topics. The two books by Sir W. Ivor Jennings, *The British Constitution* (Cambridge University Press, 1958), and *The Queen's Government* (Pelican Books, 1960), are a sound introduction to the subject. The collected essays edited by Lord Campion in *Parliament — a Survey* (Allen and Unwin Ltd., 1963) make a stimulating study; narrower in scope, but still useful is *British Government since 1918* (Allen and Unwin Ltd., 1950), another group of essays edited by Lord Campion. As a complement to these mainly academic studies Lord Morrison's *Government and Parliament* (O.U.P., 3rd Edition, 1964) gives an interesting insight into some of the practical problems of government. Another book springing from practical experience is *Thoughts on the Constitution* (Oxford University Press, 1953) by the Right Honourable L. S. Amery. The book's value, however, does not rest purely on the author's personal experience of politics. He has related this experience to his own conception of the way in which Government may be the most efficiently conducted; it is from this constructive approach to practice and theory that his well-known scheme for a smaller Cabinet resulted. Finally, *Some Problems of the Constitution* (Hutchinson and Co. Ltd., Revised Edition, 1961) by G. Marshall and G. C. Moodie provides useful supplementary material to a basic study of constitutional topics.

The books mentioned so far might well be consulted on the specialist topics too, but there are of course many books on particular aspects of government. On the monarchy (Chapter 1) there are, in particular, Sir Charles Petrie's *The Modern British Monarchy* (Eyre and Spottiswoode Ltd., 1961), and D. Morrah's *The Work of the Queen* (Kimber and Co. Ltd., 1958). For a detailed study of the recent influence of the monarch in constitutional matters the biography of King George VI (Macmillan and Co. Ltd., 1958) by Sir John Wheeler-Bennett is most useful. From the wealth of material on the historical development of the monarchy it would be invidious to single out one specialist book rather than another. For a wide view of a long and formative period, however, E. N. William's *The 18th Century Constitution 1688–1815* (Cambridge University Press, 1960) is valuable. For background knowledge of a much longer period, Sir David Keir's *Constitutional History of Modern Britain 1485–1959* (A. & C. Black Ltd., 6th Edition, 1960) is most informative.

The subject-matter of Chapters 2–5 (The Cabinet, Prime Minister, Ministers of the Crown, Civil Servants, and the relationship of Government to the citizen) is closely interrelated. Several of the books mentioned earlier, such as Lord Morrison's *Government and Parliament*, L. S. Amery's *Thoughts on the Constitution*, and *Parliament — a Survey*, edited by Lord Campion, all have relevance to this section. In addition J. P. Mackintosh's *The British Cabinet* (Stevens and Sons Ltd., 1962) is a most illuminating description of the way in which the British Cabinet works, and the influences to which it is subject. For the specialist, *Cabinet Government* (Cambridge University Press, 3rd Edition, 1959) by Sir W. Ivor Jennings is essential. The interesting and indeed crucial problem of the extent to which Cabinet action can be influenced by opinion outside its own ranks is considered, directly or indirectly, in many other books. Amongst these J. D. Stewart's *British Pressure Groups* (Oxford University Press, 1958), R. T. McKenzie's *British Political Parties* (Heinemann, 2nd Edition 1963), T. A. Critchley's *The Civil Service Today* (Victor Gollancz Ltd., 1951), and G. A. Campbell's *The Civil Service in Britain* (Pelican Books, 1955) are particularly useful. The detailed study by D. N. Chester and N. Bowring, *Questions in Parliament* (Oxford — Clarendon Press, 1962), should be consulted for a full assessment of the influence of that form of Parliamentary procedure. For an examination of the functions and importance of the Prime Minister there is Byrum E. Carter's *The Office of Prime Minister* (Faber and Faber Ltd., 1956). If detailed studies of the working of Government Departments are required then the books in the New Whitehall series, published by Allen and Unwin, are very helpful. Amongst these are Sir Frank Newsam's *The Home Office* (1954), Lord Strang's *The Foreign Office* (1955), and Sir C. Jeffries' *The Colonial Office* (1956). T. E. Utley's *Occasion for Ombudsman* (Johnson, 1961) gives several interesting examples of the risk of infringement of traditional rights of citizens by the action of Government authorities. On this subject the Whyatt Report, *The Citizen and the Administration — the Redress of Grievances* (Stevens and Sons Ltd., 1961) is concise and instructive.

For Chapter 6 on the House of Commons, there is a wide choice of older books on Parliamentary procedure. They are mostly still of some value, since procedure does not change radically. Lord Campion's *An Introduction to the Procedure of the House of Commons* (Macmillan and Co. Ltd., 3rd Edition, 1958) is one of the best known and authoritative. Among recent books Eric Taylor in *The House of Commons at Work* (Pelican Books, 5th Edition, 1963) and Peter Richards in *Honourable Members* (Faber and Faber Ltd., 1959) contrive to deal with intricate subject-matter without crushing interest with a weight of knowledge. On Parliamentary control of finance B. Chubb's *The Control of National Expenditure* (Oxford University Press, 1952), and P. Einzig's *The Control of the Purse* (Secker and Warburg, 1959) are excellent. K. C. Wheare's *Government by Committee* (Oxford — Clarendon Press, 2nd Edition, 1955) is most instructive on the work of Committees inside and outside Parliament. *Parliament at Work* (Stevens and Sons Ltd., 1962) by A. H. Hanson and H. V. Wiseman describes Parliamentary procedure by a series of ably chosen excerpts from proceedings of the House of Commons. Finally, although no book on Parliament is likely to be entirely comprehensive, *Parliament* (Cambridge University Press, 2nd Edition, 1961) by Sir Ivor Jennings is probably the nearest to being so.

Voting systems (Chapter 7) are the special interest of the Electoral Reform Society (Albany Institute, Creek Road, London, S.E. 8) which supplies pamphlets on application. Books on the subject are not common but there is *Voting in Democracies* (Faber

M

and Faber Ltd., 2nd Edition, 1959) by Miss Enid Lakeman, who is director and secretary of the Electoral Reform Society, and J. D. Lambert. D. E. Butler's *The Electoral System in Britain since 1918* (Oxford University Press, 1963) is a useful description of the existing system.

The House of Lords (Chapter 8) has received scant attention as a specialist topic. References to its value will be found in the general books mentioned at the beginning of the book-list. In particular, the account of the House of Lords by F. W. Lascelles in *Parliament — a Survey* (Allen and Unwin Ltd., 1955) should be consulted. There is also *Shall we reform the Lords?* (Falcon Press Ltd., 1948) by Martin Lindsay, and the Fabian pamphlet No. 305 *The Privy Council as a Second Chamber* by Anthony Wedgwood Benn. The fullest study, however, is that by P. A. Bromhead, *The House of Lords and Contemporary Politics, 1911–1957* (Routledge and Kegan Paul Ltd., 1958).

There are several excellent books on the working of the Judiciary. *The Criminal Law* (Pelican Books, 3rd Edition, 1963) and *The Magistrates' Courts* (Pelican Books, 1955), both by F. T. Giles, give useful accounts of procedure. The role of the Justice of the Peace in the system is considered in more detail in L. Page's *Justice of the Peace* (Faber and Faber Ltd., 2nd Edition, 1947) and in F. Milton's *In Some Authority* (Pall Mall Press Ltd., 1959). The work of the other laymen in the system, the jurors, is described and discussed in Lord Devlin's *Trial by Jury* (Stevens and Sons Ltd., 1956). The difficult but important matter of disentangling the principles under-lying the judicial system was attempted in Professor A. V. Dicey's famous analysis of the Rule of Law in *The Law of the Constitution* (Macmillan and Co. Ltd., 10th Edition, 1959). These views have since been strongly challenged by Sir Ivor Jennings in *The Law and the Constitution* (University of London Press, 5th Edition, 1959). A study of the latter, in particular, will show how difficult it is to be both accurate and enlightening in defining the principles on which the English judicial system is based. R. M. Jackson's *The Machinery of Justice* (Cambridge University Press, 4th Edition, 1964) makes interesting reading on the matter of the relationship of the Executive to the Judiciary, particularly in the section which considers the idea of a Ministry of Justice. Other recent assessments of the relationship between the Executive and the Judiciary are to be found in *Protection from Power under*

English Law (Stevens and Sons Ltd., 1957) by Lord MacDermott and in the publications of *Justice* (Stevens and Sons Ltd.).

The new developments in the structure and finance of local government were discussed in Chapter 10. So far as I know the recent proposals have not been considered in books yet. The details of the proposed changes are contained in the publications of Her Majesty's Stationery Office. The White Paper (Cmnd. 1562, 1961) gives the Government's views on the proposals of the Royal Commission on Greater London. The report of the Commission is contained in Cmnd. 1164, 1960. The reports of the Special Area Commissions are published as their work is completed. So far draft proposals and reports on the Tyneside, West Midlands, and Wales have been published (November, 1962). For those wishing to study why these proposed changes have become necessary there are several books which give reliable descriptions of the structure and functions of local government authorities. J. H. Warren's *Municipal Administration* (Sir Isaac Pitman and Sons Ltd., 2nd Edition, 1954), L. Golding's *Local Government* (English Universities Press, 1959), W. E. Jackson's *Local Government in England and Wales* (Pelican Books, 2nd Edition, 1959), and *Local Government in England and Wales* (Home University Library, 2nd Edition, 1953) by Sir J. Maud and S. E. Finer, all give ample material on these matters. *Servant of the County* (Dennis Dobson, 1956) by M. Cole is an informative account of the work of a London county councillor, of especial interest in view of the proposed changes in the London area.

Authors have been understandably reluctant to commit themselves to print on the subject of the rapid movement of so many former British dependencies towards self-government (Chapter 11). The success of the transition is less certain than its speed. Many problems remain unresolved and balanced assessment is peculiarly difficult. J. Strachey's *The End of Empire* (Victor Gollancz Ltd., 1959) is possibly the best attempt to fill this gap. There are, too, a few books which are helpful in showing the general pattern followed in granting self-government. Amongst these are J. Coatman's *The British Family of Nations* (George Harrap and Co. Ltd., 1950), Sir Ivor Jennings' *The Approach to Self-Government* (Cambridge University Press, 1956), M. Wight's *The Development of the Legislative Council 1606–1945* (Faber and Faber Ltd., 1947), and Sir C. Jeffries' *The Colonial*

Office (Allen and Unwin Ltd., 1956). *West Africa and the Commonwealth* (Pelican Books, 1957) by D. Austin is an attempt to describe the constitutional developments in that area with a sense of immediacy which is apt to be lacking in the purely academic approach. For those with a special interest in the legal background of the Commonwealth relationship two books by K. C. Wheare, *The Statute of Westminster and Dominion Status* (Oxford University Press, 5th Edition, 1953), and *The Constitutional Structure of the Commonwealth* (Oxford — Clarendon Press, 1960) are useful.

Chapter 12, on the strengths and weaknesses of the British constitution, was based on the evidence contained in the previous chapters so that it does not merit a separate book-list. It is worth pointing out, however, that in forming a balanced opinion of the present constitutional position the books by Sir Ivor Jennings should be consulted. J. P. Mackintosh's *The British Cabinet* is also extremely useful, not merely on the specific subject of the Cabinet itself, but also for the convincing way in which he depicts the atmosphere of modern government in Britain. The value of the many excellent radio talks on recent developments in the constitution ought not to be overlooked. The reprinting of the talks in *The Listener* gives a second chance of contact with the ideas put forward. K. C. Wheare's six lectures on *Legislatures* (reprinted in *The Listener*, issues of November 3rd–December 8th, 1955) with its lively and shrewd analysis of constitutional matters is a conspicuous example of the many instructive talks given in recent years. The value of journals in the study of the British constitution is enhanced by the rapidity of change. It is well known that books can only attempt to describe the constitution as it was, not as it is. In this situation the specialised studies which appear in periodicals such as *Parliamentary Affairs* (published by the Hansard Society) are particularly useful for their authoritative treatment of developments almost as they occur. Occasionally, too, *Public Law* (published by Stevens and Sons Ltd.) has articles of relevance to general constitutional development though the main interest is concentrated on specifically legal matters. No bibliography would be complete without mention of the abundant source material to be found in the publications of Her Majesty's Stationery Office. Apart from official reports and similar material the Stationery Office also publishes in pamphlet or book form concise statements of factual information on governmental matters. The annual edition of *Britain: an Official Handbook* compiled by the Central Office is particularly useful for reference for students new to the subject. A wisely chosen selection of documents as an accompaniment to constitutional studies is to be found in G. H. L. Le May's *British Government 1914–1953; Select Documents* (Methuen and Co. Ltd., 1955). Finally, it may be worth reminding school readers of the many excellent articles on the subject of government to be found in sections of the national Press. They are an invaluable means of becoming well-informed on a subject where alertness to new developments in governmental practice is essential for the student at any level.

Index

PRINTED IN GREAT BRITAIN
BY ROBERT MACLEHOSE AND CO. LTD
THE UNIVERSITY PRESS, GLASGOW

DATE DUE

AP 22'66			
FE 2 '67			
AP 7'67			
AUG 3 0 1967 RESERVED			
SEMINAR 10 Jan 225			
FEB 16 1968 RESERVED			
APR 8 10 P.M.			
APR 14 6 P.M.			
APR 23 7 P.M.			
DEPT. OCT 14 1968			
MY 14'69			
DE 14'70			
GAYLORD			PRINTED IN U.S.A.